# The Shop on High Street

Souchou Yao

# The Shop on High Street

## At Home with Petite Capitalism

palgrave
macmillan

Souchou Yao
Researcher and Critic
Sydney, Australia

ISBN 978-981-15-2030-3 ISBN 978-981-15-2031-0 (eBook)
https://doi.org/10.1007/978-981-15-2031-0



This Palgrave Macmillan imprint is published by the registered company Springer Nature Singapore Pte Ltd.
The registered company address is: 152 Beach Road, #21-01/04 Gateway East, Singapore 189721, Singapore

# Preface

Ethnography is inescapably self-ethnography. The participant-observation method demands the ethnographer to be physically *there*, in the place where she has chosen to do fieldwork. A lot of anthropological work, from the first page, take the reader right in the field—a healing ritual, a tribal festival, a yam harvest, that fill the description. But a certain formalism, a certain decorum, makes an anthropologist write herself out. In the past, this was very much the norm. There were exceptions. Clifford Geertz begins his 1973 essay 'Deep play: notes on the Balinese cockfight': 'Early in April of 1958, my wife and I arrived, malarial and diffident, in a Balinese village we intended as anthropologists, to study.'[1] A quotidian, personal note that opens up an intricate study of a social practice at the heart of Balinese culture. One might ask: the date—'Early in April of 1958', the health and mood of Geertz and his wife—'malarial and diffident': do they need to be there in a 'social science' undertaking? The insertion of the self in the ethnography poses less of a controversy now.[2] But this has not been a totally liberating experience for the anthropologist. For self-ethnography imposes its own stricture in form and in expression. The issue of truth, the issue of what one sees and records and of what one remembers: they are still the pin-prickling reminder of how the ethnography is conceived and should be written.

Autoethnography is not freedom partly because there is a good deal of the awkwardness of emotional exposure. At times, it seems a bad taste to talk about oneself and one's family in forbiddingly intimate details. Why put it on the poor reader? At worst, it is a case of the ethnographer presuming too much. She must believe her story is worth telling, that her personal recollection illustrates a social or philosophic truth and, if she is daring, that her story contributes to the advancement of an academic discipline.

But then every act of writing is a kind of presumption. Speaking of ethnographies, one that begins with 'Early in April of 1958, my wife and I arrived, malarial and diffident ...', or one more conventionally with 'Complex and protracted mortuary ceremonies follow the deaths of senior men among the Yako of Eastern Nigeria', believes itself to be important and pursuing a useful argument.[3] Each handles the autobiographical elements differently, but they are there. With autoethnography self-revelation is very much at the heart of it; it is the price of getting the writing job done. The charge of personalism is easier to counter when we remember everyone has a story to tell, including the anthropologists. Ask any refugees or migrants; their life stories are as commonplace as they are full of pain and unexpected encounters. For them as for us, what appears to be self-revelation is nothing more than the willingness to remember. And the task of remembering is often psychologically forbidding: why drag up the past when the present demands all the effort and inner resources one can muster in the business of living? This, I rather think, is not vastly from the self-ethnographer and the task she faces: autobiography complicates things; the meandering narrative compromises the claim for objectivity and truth.

On the question of truth—of the unreliability of memory—one goes back to the idea of human being as givers of meaning to things. Truth has its force of validity; it is also something of the mind and the body. For Merleau-Monty, if I am a consciousness that embraces and constitutes the world, that consciousness is also something of the bodily senses, of the hard materiality of existence. Mind and body both made possible the way we perceive the world and reflect on the meaning of our existence. In Merleau-Monty's words:

> Reflection does not withdraw from the world towards the unity of consciousness as the world's basis; it steps back to watch the forms of transcendence fly up like sparks from a fire; it slackens the intentional threads which attach us to the world and thus brings them to our notice; it alone is consciousness of the world because it reveals that world as strange and paradoxical.[4]

Those self-ethnographers plagued with doubts do well to take heed of this remarkable passage from *Phenomenology of Perception*. Our perceptions and remembrance do not make for the neat formalism of conventional storytelling. A self-narrative to be free from the 'strange' and the 'paradoxical' does not do justice to the harsh reality and happy lyricism of everyday life.

In 2012 Mr Tan our family solicitor finally sold the terrace house my parents had brought for their retirement, and the ledgers and documents were returned to us. This book has its origin in this simple event. My father had kept a diary right until the last months before he died. Over the years I had spoken to my mother about the family business, especially during those years I was away at the university. I had been gently prodded by my siblings into get this project going; it was they who took me to visit this Uncle and that Aunt who remember our parents still.

The writing had been much caught up with how to strike a balance between self-revelation and the narrative protocol. What have gone into it are what had actually happened, though not all fact and events, however interesting and true, are in this book. This is a matter of rhetorical flow, as much as that of narrative economy.

I have made each chapter more or less complete in itself. This makes for easier reading by those who do not wish to cover the whole book. The result is some repetitions of characters and theoretical issues that run through some chapters. As for the use of the female personal pronoun: the shopkeepers we knew and did businesses with were all men, so were most of our customers, so it is dissonant to use 'she' when referring to anyone of them.

All money values are in Malaysian ringgit. In the late 1970s, the period of the ethnography, the exchange rate was about 1 MYR to 0.4 USD.[5]

Sydney, Australia — Souchou Yao

## Notes

1. 'Deep Play: Notes on the Balinese Cockfight', in Clifford Geertz, *The interpretation of Culture*. NY: Basic Books, 1973, pp. 412–453.
2. See Geertz's meditation on this issue: 'The state of the art'. In Clifford Geertz. *Available Light: Anthropological Reflections on Philosophic Topics*. Princeton: Princeton University Press, 2002, pp. 80–133.

3. The latter quote comes from, Daryll Forde, 'Death and Succession: an analysis of Yoko mortuary ceremony', in Max Gluckman (ed), *Essays on the Ritual of Social Relations*, Manchester: Manchester University Press, 1962, p. 89.
4. Maurice Merleau-Ponty, *Phenomenology of Perception*. Translated by Colin Smith, London: Routledge, 1962, p. xv.
5. https://fxtop.com/en/historical-currency-converter. Accessed 19 September, 2019.

## Bibliography

Geertz, Clifford. 1973. 'Deep Play: Notes on the Balinese Cockfight'. In *The interpretation of Culture*. NY: Basic Books, 1973, pp. 412–453.

——— 2002. *Available Light: Anthropological Reflections on Philosophic Topics*. Princeton: Princeton University Press.

Merleau-Ponty, Maurice. 1962. *Phenomenology of Perception*. Translated by Colin Smith. London: Routledge.

### Internet Resources

Source: https://fxtop.com/en/historical-currency-converter. Accessed 19 September, 2019.

# Contents

CHAPTER 1

# Petite Capitalism: What Drives It?

It was a task to teach me responsibility, and how to be a part of the team. See, you do it this way, my father would say. You have to use the fingers of both hands, and you have to stroke each note, each sheet of the bills. He was patient and unhurried, and I was a quick learner. The trick, I discovered, was to hold the notes between the thumb and the index finger of both hands just tight enough to 'feel' the papery surface. To start counting, the right index finger flipped up a note, the left index finger and thumb gripped and gave it a light rub to make sure it's a single sheet. It called for coordination and dexterity of the fingers. Later when I got good at it, I could do it blind, without looking. With a slab of ten or fifty-ringgit bills, I put the notes through the deft fingering, while my head made the silent count: 'One, two, three, four, five, six ....' Each count summoned, as it would for the blind, the grimy feel of an old note, and once in a while, the surprising crispness of a new one. The feel was everything: the worn notes a soft drag on the fingertips, the new notes a coarse tingling, like pages of a new book.

I did this each evening with my father, when we emptied the cash register and entered the daily take in the ledger. I had a lot of practice; I honed my skills through the high school years and later when I came home during the university vacation. It is an art all but useless in these days of internet banking and cashless transaction. Yet, the habit has been drilled into me, and I find it hard to shake it off. Decades on, in another country, it astonished my fellow shoppers when, given a bundle of bills at



S. Yao, *The Shop on High Street*,
https://doi.org/10.1007/978-981-15-2031-0_1

the Woolworth supermarket cash-out, I began to wet my fingers and fly through the notes right at the counter. The checkout lady stared, and the people in the queue were amazed. Deeply embarrassed I instantly stopped. I was sure everyone was sniggering at me, at my skill that tagged me as a Scrooge or one with a vulgar fondness for money. I grabbed the money and, near the trollies outside, took a deep breath to recoup my dignity. Secretly, though, I could not help but feel a sense of pride at the skill so quaintly out of date. It was a social blunder, but it called up for me the golden hours I spent working with my father on the great ironwood table at the High Street shop. I was never so close to my father as I was during those evening hours. We counted the take for the day, we went through the ledgers and we were two comrades behind the barricade facing the common enemy. Our hopes were adhered to those precious notes. They were, like the family, the bastion against the duplicitous world. As I reached the final note, I felt I had entered the centre of a mystery which had consumed my parents and left its mark on their children.

This book tells the story of a small family business, so it begins with money. Simmel in *The Philosophy of Money* sees money as a modernizing force that levels out the 'subjective interest' of a buyer or a seller, and divides the values of goods into 'objective units of measurement'.[1] Money drives the small family business, and you get it right when you read Simmel next to, say, Dickens' *Dombey and Son*. Both are about the power of money; and Dickens' novel spins a tragic tale of wealth and commerce—and of Mr Dombey's sickly son who fails to bear the weight of the family legacy. Money enters the family, and fear and corruption do their devil's work.

But this came to me later. In those years in the seventies, money was everything to us. Living in a Chinese shophouse was a lesson in the value of money. Like the poor, we did not rave about the moral hollowness of money, a presumption we could not afford. What paid the bills, what kept the wolf—and the creditors, more literally—from the door, and later what sustained my brothers and I at the university, were those grimy notes. Practicality ruled the way we thought about money. The lack of it, not its corrupting power, was the source of our worries. For money never seemed to stay long enough with us to cause us problems, to stir up the moral issues.

Each evening after we had entered the day's taking in the ledger, my father would consult the account books and allocated the money accordingly. This 800 ringgit would go to Hegemeyer, the wholesaler of the ever popular Eagle Medical Oil; the Tiger Balm salesman was coming the next day, this 1,000 ringgit would be for him; the rest was to be deposited in the bank for the cheques my father had written. Putting the neat bundles of cash in the safe was the first step of a vanishing act. Money felt to us like the stuff of floating life, to use a Chinese expression, short-lived and without substance. But it dominated our lives; it measured our successes; and the lack of it gauged our failures.

Against these sorry tales, what of the happier ones? I suppose they count, too, as part of the story Chinese petite capitalism. My parents had, in all appearances, a good marriage. There were devoted to each other, and they had made their marriage work. They squabbled about this and that, but they were a team in raising the family and in running the shop. There was love in the family. Against the moral shambles and financial shortfalls, there were triumphs and ambitions realized. Ours were tiger parents before the term was invented. They invested in their children's education. Three of the five children went to the university. Our parents made us study hard, with the refrain: have a good education; no one can take that away from you. Against the gloom of petite capitalism, I am glad how things have turned out for me and my siblings. I have hung on to the memory of the family business and of my father's deft financial management that gave the family a modicum of prosperity. We were, in the miracle of miracles, realizations of a cliché. For its many shortcomings, Chinese petite capitalism felt to us like a blessing. Sometimes I even think we were lucky to be born in a Chinese shophouse, with parents as astute and undefeatable as ours. We have thrived and we have been made prosperous. But our parents barely survived it.

The 'petite' of petite capitalism suggests sins and deficiencies of various kinds. 'Petite' points to the 'littleness' of a shop's capital, the 'littleness' of its scale of production, the 'littleness' of its level of profit and cash saving. Petite capitalists are small merchants, self-sustaining peasants, tradesmen, weavers, ironsmiths, the self-employed. The conventional terms are 'petty capitalism' and 'petty capitalists', each with its unhappy prefix. Petty gives petty capitalism unflattering connotations: conservative, traditional, lacking in innovation. And with 'petty capitalists', you are aware of the social disparagement: they are regressive, they tend to identity with the status quo and those in power. In either case, it is a quick descent from 'small' or 'quaint and attractive', to 'contemptibly trivial'.[2] With petty capitalism, it is hard not to associate it with another term of denigration: 'petty bourgeoisie' or the adjective 'petty bourgeois'. Raymond Williams' in *Keywords* gives a historical account of the term 'bourgeois'. It had its origin as a 'juridical category' of residents in French feudal society, whose 'stable and solvent' mode of life invited the aristocratic judgement of 'mediocrity'.[3] From the French usage is emerged the current social disdain for the bourgeoisie—the classic middle class—with their small-mindedness, philistine taste, self-obsession. The petite bourgeoisie—and the petite capitalists—are not passionate, romantic figures given to wild speculations and lurid fantasies.

It is quite a lot to put on the modest family shop and the people who own and run it. The question is with the littleness in all its aspects: what kind of capitalism is petty capitalism?

For a start, let us revert it back the more useful 'petite'. 'Petite' of the original French describes the economic form; it is more moderate while it retains a touch of the derogatory. 'Petite capitalism' allows us to examine the structural limits of the small family enterprise and reminds us to spurn the easy vilification.

When we look around any town or city, petite capitalism seems everywhere. It is the all-hours corner shops, the food takeaways, the Asian groceries, the shoe repairs and tin smiths and hawkers in the streets, it is the family-run small workshops making mobile phone covers, rubber slippers and plastic indoor plants at the back alleys of any Third World city. With these businesses, the owner-operator is the family whose members work for free, they do not draw wages and there is no talk of opportunity costs of this 'free labour'. Besides the family, the lifeline of petite capitalism is the network of friends and kin; these are its customers, its labour recruiters, its money lenders, its marketing agents. This marriage of social relations and their economic use is complicated and alluring. For people like my father, it called up the practices in the past when financial dealings were personal, when economic affairs were conducted with an awareness of their impact on others. With petite capitalism, economic affairs are more often than not social affairs. Contemporary petite capitalism is a boilerplate capitalism where making profits and making—and keeping—friends are deemed possible.

Maybe petite capitalism is a kind of pariah capitalism, not quite the real thing. My father spoke of the village way of doing business. For him doing business with kin involved a certain ethics; you did not apply the law of the jungle when you dealt with your relatives. He believed business transactions should be ethical and socially considered.

The anthropologist James Scott roots for the petite bourgeoisie. Scott casts a wide net; petite bourgeoisie include the army of shopkeepers, smallholding peasant, hawkers and peddlers, self-employed professionals; petite capitalists all. He praises their sense of autonomy; he sees them as fighting for freedom against the state and its public bureaucracies. Their need for independence and for the freedom to work in their own time, in their own place, makes them 'anarchist heroes'.[4]

Petite capitalists are also praised in other terms. Instead of 'heroic rebelliousness', Alan and Josephine Smart credit petite capitalists with efficiency and flexibility, qualities that earn their enterprises a place in the global economy. The Smarts are concerned with small-scale export-oriented manufacturers, larger and grander than the corner shops and takeaways. Nonetheless they all share similar social and cultural characters. With petite capitalist enterprises, the owner-operator and labour are congealed in a single institution, the family. Or, as the Smarts write, 'Petite capitalists regularly operate in the ambiguous boundaries between capital and labor, cooperation and exploitation, family and economy, tradition and modernity, friends and competitors.'[5] The advantages of these family-owned manufacturers are clear.

> Small entrepreneurs can operate in a global economy in ways that would not have been feasible a few decades ago. … Brokerage across borders provides opportunities that appeal particularly to those with little capital but high risk tolerance. At the same time, international migration and study abroad create kin and friendship ties that can facilitate taking advantage of opportunities created by local difference.[6]

In this depiction, petite capitalist enterprises are efficient and innovative, where the traditional is in sync with the modern and the contemporary. The whole family works together in harmony and observes no conflict or contradiction.

Yet structural limitation and financial shortfalls are the bird's heartbeat of petite capitalism. Rest your fingers there, and you can feel the pulsating vulnerability that plagues every small family business. My siblings and I had lived through the disasters and the prodigious hope of a Chinese shophouse. Sometimes I think a lot of the good stories about petite capitalism are bunk. At any rate, you can approach it any way you like: as a nest of anarchy, as an efficient flexible economic formation, as a place of family love and collective striving. But what is left out are the emotional costs of those working and living in it, and the fact petite capitalism is prone to failure.

The Chinese or East Asian communities' commercial genius is so legendary that it comes across as an Orientalist fantasy. Who would want to disparage the financial success of the Asian model minority, as they are called in the United States? But then who would care to know the hand-to-mouth existence that goes on in an Asian corner shop or takeaway? Look deep enough, however, and you'll find plenty that satisfies the pessimists. The bad story of petite capitalism often tells the wrong investment decisions, the struggle in the family over control and ownership, the infighting that causes the demise of the enterprise itself. But these are soap-opera stuff compared with what is the truly tragic. If petite capitalism is a form of capitalism, however distorted and unformed it tends to be, then it also falls prey to the evolutionary processes that affect capitalism as a whole. Capitalism is continuously transforming itself, both voluntarily and forced on it by wider structural circumstances. Even the modest High Street shop could not escape this fundamental truth. We had faced the boom and bust of the wider economy, and we had kept an eye on the changing opportunities in order not to miss out. As I try to understand what happened to our family business, I find an echo in *The Communist Manifesto*, and in Schumpeter's thesis of 'creative destruction', works that lay out the ever transformative nature of capitalist production. Nothing stood still. We thought the High Street shop should not have failed. After all we had worked hard, we had been a team, and our father had schemed and planned to prop up the business. We didn't deserve to fail, when others less tenacious than us had succeeded and thrived.

And we had more to lose than others. We knew it was a dangerous game to compare ourselves with others. However, as far back I could remember, everything about the family business, everything about our collective labour, had this singular quality: the need to show the world who we were and what we were made of. My father talked of giving the family a more secure financial future. He was thinking of the family, but he was also, in a sense, thinking of himself. He wanted the family to prosper, and his children to be educated, but he also needed to show the world he could be more than a shopkeeper. The social disparagement of the petite bourgeoisie runs deep.

My father, in the way of encouragement, urged us to study hard, to show *them* we were from a good family. But who were *them* to whom we had to account for our life except ourselves? As for my father, he seemed to be bedevilled by the feeling that he had somehow failed to measure up to the standards of his wealthier kin and associates. It was a mixture of truth and self-perception—and even a touch of fantasy. But it explains his restless ambitions and his need to seize the opportunities that rewarded the bold and the nimble-minded.

Chinese immigrants took their traditional medicine with them wherever they went. The ancient healing art was a part of their cultural heritage; when sick they wanted to avail themselves of a cure they had enjoyed in the home country. The feel of the doctor's hand on the pulse, the solicitous tone of his voice, his sensitive probing of the symptoms, and later, the pure bitterness of the herbal brew—they were familiar and reassuring. It was emotional therapy met medical prognosis and cure.

When my grandfather, a Hong Kong-trained herbalist, arrived in the 1930s in Ipoh, a rich mining town in the Perak state, British Malaya, he was one of the few learned men in the community. He was sought after for his medical skill and other services. As my grandmother told it, during a joyful event like a wedding he would be asked to choose a propitious date for the ceremony. And when a baby was born, the parents would approach him to pick a good name—'Big-Prosperity' for the plump male tot, 'Fragrant-Jade' for the baby girl sure to grow up into a beauty. Afterwards, he would be fighting the happy couple over the 'red packet' good luck money they pressed on him to accept. He made a bit of money, so it seemed. He later opened a pawn shop which had a liquor licence, and the corner of the shop became a bar of sort, serving beer and reconstituted brandy and whiskey for poor Indian workers. From Chinese medicine he had branched out into the lending business and selling shoddy alcohol beverages, because there was more money in them.

The family legend stretches far back, but grandmother tended to get a bit tongue-tied when she got too close to those years. Grandfather, she said, was restless, the cover-all word that describes his temperament; he was a man not easy to please. I had in my head the image of staid healer, immersed in tradition, deep in the communal affairs; but grandmother's telling dispelled the cliché. But what kind of man was he? She once told me that grandfather had a mistress, a local Chinese woman, a young school teacher; and grandmother had threatened to go back to China where grandfather had bought land and built a grand house. She also told me her husband had cared deeply about what happened in China; and he had taken part in the boycotting of Japanese goods in Malaya when Japan invaded the Chinese mainland in 1937. I was a little stunned and puzzled. A Chinese doctor, well-read and with a social reputation to match;

a loving husband who shacked up with a young woman from the tropics; a traditionalist and a nationalist with modern thinking: they all described the man. Grandmother and I talked over the years, but the veil over my grandfather was not lifted.

A few years back I took my children to see *Once Upon a Time in China* when it had just come out in a local cinema in Singapore, the city where I had taken a university job. And I thought: grandfather would be just one more generation after Master Wong Feihong; he would have shared Wong's values and nationalist sentiments. *Once Upon a Time in China* converted my kids Akaash and Neena to life-time fans of Jet Li and his martial art epics. In the film, Wong Feihong, the kung fu master and traditional healer, is a bold and wise figure, expert in the 'no shadow kick' of the Wing Chun school, doing battle with opium-trading foreign devils and Chinese religious cult followers alike. Wong is even made to fall in love with Thirteen Aunt, his stepmother's youngest sister, a San Francisco-educated, skirt-wearing modern woman, but the incestual joke was lost to my kids. I told them Master Wong was closest to what their great-grandfather was like. Like Master Wong, he was a traditional healer edging towards modernity in the pre-war years of the late 1930s. He had found love outside marriage, and he was a fervent cultural nationalist. In some ways grandfather's temperament explained something of my father. For he too was 'restless'; and like grandfather he was confident and ambitious, yet with a keen eye for the unexpected and the perilous.

I was close to my father. From my teenage years until the time I left for university in Adelaide, Australia, I worked in the shop and he gave me what jobs I could do. I helped keep the accounts and handle the cash. He wanted to toughen me and to give me a feel of the herbal business. I also believe he was trying to cultivate a father-and-son rapport he didn't have with his father. Like people self-taught—he was taken off from the second year in high school to help in the Ipoh pawnshop—he had a fondness for reading and learning. His mind was fed by books from the World Bookshop in Petaling Street in Chinatown, the popular purveyor of traditional and modern texts from Hong Kong and China. When he talked, he gave the impression of trying out ideas, to see if what he had read had any purchase on his present life. He was a person whose character implied a certain fluidity. I shall in the following pages describe him as an 'innovative conservative', a 'petite capitalist with a modern outlook', a 'figure of male authority who valued daughters over sons'—labels that best describe the man I knew.

My father was a sticker for ethics, for what he called proper behaviour, which he brought into all his dealings. It was for him a matter of practice and personal conviction. His counsel of the importance of honesty, trustworthiness and respectability was drummed into me. In my teenage years, my response was often a sense of cynical incredulity. He spoke of trust and honesty, but his was a world of cut-throat competition and not infrequently, distrust and betrayal. So my father's approach to business seemed near impossible. It is as if he wanted the material gain, but he also yeaned for the approval of others. Unless, of course, personal trust and social approval have economic significance, something useful in business. In that case, social capital is just another form of capital, one from which a person can expect to draw benefits from it over time. After my first-year at university, I had the language: the market is objective; self-interests and competition are natural. There's no bad behaviour in the Smithian realm of freedom to trade.

For more than 2000 years, the bible of Chinese medicine has been the *Huangdi Neijing*, The Yellow Emperor's Inner Canon. The text is an elaborate thesis on the human body, laying out the movements of the yin and yang, and the alignments of the five elements—wood, fire, earth, metal, water, as the determinants of one's state of health. It describes the use of acupuncture and moxibustion in achieving the yin-yang harmony in the human body. *Huangdi Neijing* was written during the Shang Dynasty (1600–1040 BC); the text is esoteric, its medical and philosophic reasonings impenetrable but it had a huge impact on Chinese medical thinking. Like others of his time, my father used two works that were more accessible: *Shanghan Lun*, The Treatise on Cold Injuries, written in the late Han Dynasty (206 BC–220 AD), and the *Bencao Gengmu*, The Compendium of Materia Medica, written by the court physician Li Shizhen in the mid-Ming Dynasty (1518–1593). These became popular to contemporary readers when the Commercial Press of Shanghai brought out various editions during the thirties, each updated and simplified, and added with modern commentaries.

My father's copy of *Shanghan Lun* is the 1950 edition, which he kept in the shelf next to the account ledgers and Dale Carnegie's *How to Win Friends and Influence People* (in Chinese). The Commercial Press had slimmed down the original and rearranged the taxonomy of illnesses and cures for easier reading. This was the text he consulted most of the time. Beside *Shanghan Lun*, there were books and pamphlets on Chinese healing that came out of Hong Kong and China. These were cheap and written in colloquial Chinese, a boon to self-taught students of Chinese medicine. To aid rote learning, the ailments and prescriptions were set in rhyme, the sing-song made them easy to remember. Chinese medicine may be an ancient art, but the profession itself could be fairly democratic.[7] During my father's time in the seventies, Chinese healers in Malaysia were largely self-taught. Most, with their small consultation fees and low-volume herbal trade, did not make money—especially those in the villages who practised in the sundry shops they owned.

Throughout my high school years, the medical texts looked down at me with their unyielding mystery. I was fascinated. They presented a challenge when I had acquired some proficiency in classic Chinese from school. Hard as I tried, it was difficult to get past the jumble of elucidations and exegeses.

Take for example, the first line of *Shanghan Lun*. It reads:

Tai yang zhi wei bing, mai fu, tou xiang jiang er wu han.

The line appears under the section 'diseases relating to the greater [excessive] yang'. It is a wonder of the Chinese written script that for all the transfigurations over the ages, the words—and to a lesser extent their meanings—can still be understood today with a bit of effort. *Shanghan Lun* was written more than 2000 years ago; in the text tai yang is the sun, same as the modern term for it. We know yang also denotes the masculine element in the ying-yang binary. Yu is still the term for pulse; tou for head; tong for pain. So the modern rendering can be:

In illnesses of the greater (extreme?) yang,
the pulse is floating,
the head and nape are stiff and painful,
and [the patient] is averse to cold.

The translation comes from the internet-based Chinese Text Project.[8] It is concise, but a tad too literal. As with most classical Chinese text, there is here room for more liberal interpretations. Following the spirit of the text, the sensation of pain and coldness are more metaphysical than physical. Han is cold (in the meteorological sense), but it can also describe one's spiritual or emotional state (as in the lover's complaint, in English, 'You are a cold bastard'). A person who is averse to han does not necessarily feel the iciness in the air or for sitting under a fan after a cold bath.

More creatively, we can say: the patient's condition has risen from the poor qi or due to the lack of the yang element; both Qi and yang are metaphysical concepts. For the cure, keeping warm matters. But more so the patient should follow a 'hot' diet of toasted ginger and wine and in another realm, receive sympathy and support from the loved ones. Melancholy and poor spirits are the causes and symptoms of 'cold illnesses'. Stress and depression put you at risk of catching a cold, the so-called yuppie flu that plagues office workers in winter.

So my juvenile reading became a kind of Barthesian exercise. It is almost as if there was no final, authoritative reading; meanings were delayed until they reached another set of inferences. Whether I was right or wrong, traditional Chinese healing tends to allow a degree of freedom in the diagnosis and cure. Even my father agreed on this, if somewhat grudgingly. Everything moves quickly from the literal to the metaphorical. A han illness means avoiding coldness in all forms: no drinking of ice water, no fruits and salad, no cold bath. And it also means steering away from han-inducing situations: don't get upset, leave all stressful decision until later, and certainly a broken heart induces cold in the body and can make you sick. I am no expert in Chinese medicine. Each time I read a medical text, I have to struggle to make some headway into the elaborate metaphysis behind the exegesis and cure. On the other hand, it fascinated me as I watched my father: with each illness, he faced an array of choices in regard to the diagnosis and the prescription of cure, and his decision was nothing short of being creative. Everything depended on the patient's conditions, the doctor's diagnosis and the size of the patient's wallet.

The consultation took place at a small desk at the corner of the shop. The desk was painted yellow—a lucky colour, and next to it a few chairs where patients sat and waited for their turn. There were no receptionist and well-thumbed magazines, but there were grim-faced men and women, listless children sucking on sweets that bought good behaviour and infants swaddled in layers of flannel—even in the tropics. It was morning and more than a handful of patients had come to see the doctor. For the shop, the patients and their silent waiting were like the stock exchange signboard, an indication of what kind of day it was going to be.

Dressed in a white cotton blouse and a pair black pants, my father arrived from upstairs. He sat before the small desk and murmured a few words to the patient across. Everyone knew the drill. The patient offered her wrist, and the doctor bent his arm and rested his fingers on it. Sensing the pulse is all about the feel, a sensitive touch of the blind that reveals what a person of sight misses. To get the right 'feel', a doctor's fingers have to be firm yet delicate. My father 'listened' to the pulse, his eyes kept a faraway look. You've got a severe flu, the doctor said when he finished. She listened then broke out in a spasm of wheezing and coughing. When she recovered, the doctor lifted his voice: you are not to take showers for the next few days; you are to watch out for your stool, and no deep-fried dishes and local fruits. Then he picked up the ink brush and started to write out a prescription. Secured in her hand, the script travelled with the patient to the counter. The foreman picked it up and laid it flat on the counter and began to fill the script. On any busy morning, he staged a play of keen eyes and hands busily opening and closing the wooden chests sunken into the wall: stores of herbs, dried insects and shrivelled animal parts. Each journey from the chests brought back an amount which the foreman carefully weighed and laid on a sheet of paper. The woman eyed at the proceedings and waited.

Other times, when a patient's ailment was more serious than a flu, the doctor-patient exchange would go beyond cold showers and the bowel movement and local fruits.

Trouble in the family, a quarrel between husband and wife, parents having problems with their children can all cause a person to fall sick. Chinese medicine identifies a whole range of illnesses caused by malfunctioning of the liver: the organ that governs reasoning and emotions. Rage and mental imbalance disturb the liver functioning, delivering cold conditions that lead to headache, blurry vision and pain in the lower abdomen.

The patient Mrs Wang was a 52-year-old married woman with children. She came to see the doctor complaining of intense headache. Her heart was heavy, she said. She had no appetite, she couldn't sleep. My father gently probed: when did the head pain start? Have you always suffered from it? She started to ramble—about her weak heart, about her family problems. The doctor took note: her husband had been going out every night and came home two or three in the morning; and there were strange phone calls for him which he would not return. The doctor had heard enough—a marital strife, a husband's infidelity—and got her to stop.

The patient had expressed what was on her mind, and she had had her pulse felt, the colour of her tongue scrutinized, the fleshiness of her palm assessed. My father started to write the prescription; it included ginseng—she seemed wealthy enough to afford it, and liquorice root and dang gui and other herbs that help to restore the workings of the liver and kidneys in order to induce the flow of qi. Mrs Wang seemed calmer.

He sent her off with the instruction: take it to the counter, stew the medicine with three cups of water down to one cup. Keep warm and don't worry too much.

Across the yellow table, the doctor and patient were as partners acting out a ritual, a performance. And one could catch a good deal from the brief words and simple gestures. The strength of Chinese medicine is not coronary artery bypass or breast biopsy. It is best for treating illnesses with a social and emotional origin.[9] A good candidate for Chinese medicine, for example, is back pain due to bad posture and a variety of stressful situations, from financial worries to extended use of the computer keyboard. Whether he liked it or not, some of the extra-medical causes were brought to my father in a consultation.

The Chinese healer is a doctor, a pharmacist, a therapist, a wellness consultant. Often he is also a petite capitalist and a medicine merchant.

With Mrs Wang, my father had been brisk and business-like. He knew her reputation for loquacity, and Chinese medicine was not like the talking cure of modern psychotherapy. The 'talking cure' was left to the mediation sessions he presided over in the Hakka Association office, where couples in marital strife, borrowers and lenders of money in dispute, came to seek remedies. When the healer was also the shop owner, other calculations began to creep in. At the High Street shop, strange bedfellows are made of petite capitalism and Chinese medicine.

It has been a ponderous narrative of Chinese medicine in the setting a small family business. Thinking of the family history I feel locked in, embattled. My grandfather's beginning, the legacy he left to his eldest son, my father's own ambitions and departures—they were like the modern city to a new visitor, smooth and discernible, yet grim and hinting of secrets. The elements of our forefathers' past do not make a consistent whole. There were serendipities they could not foresee, and they often changed the direction half way down their adult years—as my father did when he gave up his medical practice.

One reason for my father's change of heart was financial. Chinese medicine rarely made much money. At the High Street shop the patients paid five ringgit each for consultation, and on a good day there would be from eight to twelve of them in the morning, with a dribble in the afternoon. The patients came because of my father's reputation and because they believed herbs were better for them than pills and injections. For most, the biggest draw card of Chinese medicine was it was cheap. A prescription costed perhaps another ten ringgit; so a visit to the Chinese healer came to around 15 ringgit, while at a clinic a doctor's consultation fee alone would be at least twice that. The slim harvest was typical of a traditional healer's earning. Yet, a medicine shop could not do without one. The healer was its brand mark, he put his stamp on its reputation and the goods it sold. What kind of medicine shop would it be without the sombre, elderly man who felt your pulse and got you to watch over the colour your stool? In any case, my father quickly coaxed his friend Master Hwang out of retirement to serve at the shop. Master Hwang was in his mid-seventies; he had studied in Hong Kong and had practised for many years in Singapore. So he was to be shop's new anchor, and to give my father time to attend to the business side of things.

The money is one thing, it is also the case that my father was unhappy with the state of his profession. It admitted too many, mostly self-taught. Anyone who had read a few simplified texts, and memorized the prescriptions, could set himself up as a Chinese doctor. The profession was getting crowded and full of amateurs, he complained. He was himself self-taught, of course. But he was different: he had read widely, and he was versed in the scholarship—he was no quack. And he was a man who listened to the BBC Chinese broadcast, and read for relaxation the wuxia novels of Louis Cha. Modern taste and learning had made him question some of his fellow practitioners.

Or maybe because he needed a change. Perhaps he was like one of those going through a mid-life crisis: any change will do as long as life is no longer the same dreary routine. There was a bit of that. Risk-taking and economic adventurism were not his way. But forces were pressing on him that made him reassess his options. In Malaysia, capitalism had come out of the history of migration of the colonial era. The coolie labourers, the shops that serve customers of all sorts, the wholesalers and trading agents of commodities—they made Malaya one of the richest colonies of the British Empire. And this history had created a particular cultural ethos among the immigrant communities, particularly the Chinese. Everything of this ethos is vulnerable, self-possessing and economically aggressive. My father and so many like him were inheritors of a cultural legacy, which they embellished with the values of personal efforts, inventiveness and imagination.

And what is imagination in this context except the effusive emanations of what drives the petite capitalist? With these emanations, imagination becomes passion, reason becomes unreason and failure turns into shame. The Chinese petite capitalists are not only creatures of dry pragmatism; they, too, have their follies and hankerings and delusions. Living with father I could not help noticing the excitement when a good deal came his way, when buying and selling of a certain commodity took on an almost magical quality.

Since passing the baton to Master Hwang, my father had not been idle. His search for contacts and opportunities had the quality of shady deals, with urgent phone calls that summoned him to a meeting at a coffee shop or at a mah-jong club, and animated talks with friends took place in the family sitting room well past midnight. Tips were exchanged and quickly responded to. The result was a series of 'trading fevers' each dealing with a particular commodity.

First was the 'streptomycin fever'.

The lorry drivers, sunburned and wearing their trademark neckerchiefs, came with their wives. They leaned against the counter, they talked about the lung sickness—tuberculosis—still ravaging their kinfolk in the hill villages in China. And they tried to bargain with my father. They feigned expertise and they examined with keen interests each aluminium strip of the drug. But my father knew it was a seller's market. The rustic buyer knew little of the medicine, except that their kin had asked for it. He had read up on it, and the supplier MS Ally Pharmacy had briefed him. Over the counter, the advantage of bulk buying—with discount—was freely dispensed, and yes, we would pack and take them to the post office and mail them to China.

This lasted for about twelve months. Then came the 'poppy husk fever'.

The poppy husks had little opium left in them. They were not in the same league as morphine and heroin; they were leftovers of opium harvest in China and the Malaysian authorities had allowed their import for use as Chinese medicine. With opiates heavily criminalized, it took certain ingenuity for consumers to find a legitimate source in the neighbourhood Chinese medicine shop. Our customers were Sikh watchmen who slept on charpoy string beds outside the bank or the pawn shop. In the solitary night hours, when the risk of robbery was low, friends got together and enjoyed a water pipe of tobacco and poppy husk. It offered solace, and perhaps reminded them of life in Punjab where farmers chewed small pills of opium to suppress appetite and overcome fatigue. The informant said: in the evening, the dahl is stewing in the clay pot, we would light up a hookah of tobacco and chandu. Sweet fire!

Coming home late at night, I sometimes stopped by and sat on a charpoy with my night-watchmen friends. Their drug-hazed contentment was contagious, and the opium discards had been put into use free from the police and social condemnation. It was certainly a better, less addictive alternative to the cheap, gut-rotting constituted brandy many night watchmen drank. It was my first introduction to a controversial subject on which everyone has an opinion, one way or the other.

Opium husk was a trade of quick turnovers. The customers came on bicycles or in a small van, each time buying two gunny sacks or more, and returned when they ran out. Then the trade died out—perhaps the night watchmen had found another source, perhaps the police had wised up; we never knew.

Each 'trading fever' gave hope to the shop's financial situation. Thanks to my father's efforts and social connections, an economic saviour was found in the commodities. Customers bought bulk, and we put a generous margin on a gross package or a gunny sack sold. All the time, there was for us a sense of waiting for the next big thing. One commodity had ceased to sell, another commodity would come to lure the customers. After the streptomycin and poppy husks, dreams rose and waned. Whether it was Tiger Balm from the Thai wholesaler who promised delivery right at the door, or sanitary napkins whose mysterious way they fell off the back of a truck we didn't want to know—miracles followed but did not last.

Fortunate for us, goods of profit were available in the shop among the repertoire of Chinese medicine—goods more enticing than the likes of streptomycin and poppy husk.

The most grandiose of the Chinese medicine shops called themselves 'pearl-ginseng- deer antler establishment'. The tonic medicines propped up the shop's name; you could not be a loser if your shop dealt in them. There were shops that sold exclusively these medicines only the rich—and the desperate—could afford. Most, like the High Street shop, peddled the ordinary day-to-day items as well as the pearl-ginseng-deer antler trinity.

Pearl lightens the skin; it makes the skin glow with lustre. (Pearl powder is the main ingredient of the face-whitening cream popular in Asia.) The medicinal pearls are the remains of those used for setting in jewellery. The best way to take them is to have them crushed and ground, and then to ingest the powder. The customers who came and asked for them were women, mostly massage parlour hostesses who had the cash and the professional vanity to keep their good looks. I remember the rush to the counter when one of them turned up. She drew attention with her bright makeup and coy demeanour, and her request was eagerly met. The box was brought out, and a portion of the precious content was weighed then ground into fine powder and laid on a sheet of fine paper and wrapped. The sale was quick, but the customer seemed to have time to chat. Pressing her arm on the sales counter, she sought assurance that what she had bought was of high quality, and that she had not over paid; and she insisted on receiving the same discount as she did last time she came. It was a satisfactory transaction all around—for the salesclerk, for the customer who bought the age-old beauty aid, for the shop that cropped an immoderate profit.

The quality and prices of ginseng vary greatly. Cheap, affordable ginseng is a misnomer. Ginseng is versatile; it is effective against high blood pressure and it heals depression and weaknesses of the brain. But the high value it fetches is also something of its rarity. Perhaps you remember Akira Kurosawa's 1975 film *Dersu Uzala*. The best quality ginseng roots are found and brought to the market by hardy huntsmen from the snowfields of Siberia and the Korean Peninsula. A certain romance is built into wild ginseng; the cheap garden-variety that fill the health food stores are farmed in the United States and China. No doubt a bit of underhandedness went on in medicine shops. My father's approach was to explain the different qualities and pricing: a 'you get what you pay for' salesmanship. The High Street shop sold both wild and farmed ginseng. Top-quality Korean ginseng was stored in air-sealed metal tins with red velvet lining: two or three roots rested inside, looking like shrivelled undersized cadavers from an ancient tomb. Over the counter each wild ginseng root fetched a price truly not for the faint-hearted.

The romance of Chinese tonic medicine really belongs to deer antler.

You can still see it in some Chinese medicine shops today in Malaysia. To preserve its efficacy, a set of deer antler is placed on a bed of cloves inside a glass case. Each horn is tied with red silk threads, which makes you think of bridal headdress in a tribal wedding. Placed prominently on the shop counter, deer antler invites admiration and impresses customers with its elegant form and beauty. Dr Subhuti Dharmananda of the Institute for Traditional Medicine, in Portland, the United States, describes deer antler's ancient origin:

> The story of deer antler can be traced back to the first Chinese Materia Medica, Shennong Bencao Jing (ca. 100 A.D.), where it is described briefly. There is also reference to earlier use of deer antler in an archaeological find (a set of silk scrolls named Wushier Bingfang, from a tomb dated 168 B.C.). However, use of antler appears to have been infrequent until the animals were raised on "deer farms" starting in the mid-16th Century in China (Ming Dynasty period). This is a time when several other cultivation and animal husbandry projects were established in support of medicine. Soon

> after, Wu Kun included a formula in his book Yi Fang Kao (Study of Prescriptions, 1584) that has inspired much work with the combination of deer antler and tortoise shell, two bone-like materials rich in gelatins.' Wu Kun's formula Gui Lu Erxian Jiao for making the firm gelatin, include the main ingredients deer antler and tortoise plastron, and some quantities of lycium fruit and ginseng.

And he lists the health benefits:

> This formula is said to replenish yin and essence, tonify qi, and strengthen yang. It is used for deficiency of kidney yin and yang, deficiency of blood and essence in the penetrating and conception vessels, with symptoms of weakness of the lower back and legs, impotence, blurred vision, etc. The penetrating vessel, (chongmai), one of the extra meridians, is referred to as the 'sea of blood.' The conception vessel (renmai), while sometimes associated with reproduction, is related to generation more broadly, including generation of blood. Tortoise shell and deer antler are said to nourish the marrow.[10]

The medicinal deer antler is actually the velvet, the cartilaginous part before it reaches calcification. Deer velvet antler is harvested from young males. It got its name from the fine, hairy surface of the horn from a beast still growing. The prong—the tine—of a velvet antler is round and sleek; from the glass case it seems to reach out as though trying to break though.

At the High Street shop, the pair of velvet antlers was attached still to the skull. It had been sitting in the case for a few months, now came the cutting and shaving of the antler velvet into flakes. We had got each interested customer to pay a deposit, and the level of commitment had been reached. A propitious day had been chosen which we wrote on a red paper stripe and pasted it on the glass casing. That day had arrived; it was Sunday morning and customers were milling around to witness the proceedings. The master grader, who had been having breakfast in the kitchen with my father, made his appearance. He cut an antler from the skull, then moved over to a long wooden bench with a cutter at the front. Everyone watched: he held firmly the antler and pressed it against the cutter, then began a steady to-and-fro motion. The first shavings were dropped onto a bamboo tray below: these were of little value, each flake white and coarse. He continued and as he reached an inch or so away from the skull, the colour of the shavings began to change. The white grey turned a red tinge: the presence of blood cells. With a pair of steel clippers, the master grader picked up a piece and holding it against the light and gave a sigh of approval. Everyone joined in: ah!

The shaving was done, and the master grader laid out the micro-thin flakes in neat piles on sheets of thin rice paper. From a ledger, my father went through the list of people who had paid the deposits and the master grader made the allotments accordingly. For a while, each precious heap stared back at you: what money could buy in the way of tonic medicine, for your health and the health of your loved ones. The pair of velvet antlers had costed almost 4,000 ringgit; it looked like we were to recoup the cost and more—perhaps three times what we had paid for them. With the generous profit, our Chinese petite capitalist dream was made real.

In many ways, Chinese shopkeepers hold many of the petite bourgeoisie attributes that James Scott speaks of with avid approval. We have witnessed their frustrations; we have been sensible to the shame and social judgement of their class positions. They suffer financial shortfalls of all kinds, and they struggle with the structural limitations of their businesses. But the petite bourgeoisie are not all lying down; as Scott points out, they rebel, they struggle against institutions and bureaucracies that exploit and oppress them. Scott's view is glossed with a certain romanticism—the making of small tradespersons into anarchists. But he is not altogether wrong. The petite capitalists of my father' generation were financially vulnerable, unlike the big wholesalers and owners of large shops. But to my mind, their weaknesses appeared to have given them a reason, a motivation for economic improvement. And they did this with a great deal of tenancy and commitment. Growing up in the High Street shop, I found my parents' diligence, their striving, their carefully guarded lives a mystery and an inspiration. I can speak of the stress and the emotional costs of living and working in a shophouse. This, however, had not been the language of my parents. Instead they talked of ethical conduct, the force of resilience, and blessings of gods and ancestors who are the final arbitrators of fate. Structural limitation was one thing; there were also personal endeavours. When my parents talked like this, it was as though profit making was an affair of the spirit—and imagination. My parents were not hard-boiled materialists: you buy and sell, and once in a while you come across a good that saves you from your financial woe, and offers perhaps a degree of excitement and fantastic hope.

We in Malaysia grew up with commodity fetishism. Rubber and tin were the mainstay of the colonial economy, both big foreign currency earners for which Britain fought a bloody counterinsurgency war during the last years of the empire.[11] Rubber and tin made prosperous the planters, the mining corporations, the agents and exporters; and wages and standard of living of the common folk rose and ebbed with the fortunes of the commodities. Children learned about rubber and tin at school, and people read in the papers how their prices spiked during the Korean and the Vietnam Wars that brought prosperity to the country. Today machinery and oil have replaced rubber and tin as Malaysia's top exports.[12] A kind of magic persists, however—magic of any goods or services that promise to deliver individual wealth and make rich the whole society. (The current candidate is real estate development.) It is capitalist myth; it is also commodity fetishism or fetishism of money. My father was no subaltern rebel; he could not resist the bewitchment that started with rubber and tin. And you might say, in the colonial divide and rule, the Chinese had been the major inheritors of Britain's commercial culture that came out of 'a nation of shopkeepers'. And what is a nation of shopkeepers but a nation of petite bourgeoise values and stringencies?

I remember each time I returned home, I would witness all the exciting goings-on at the neighbourhood. A convey of lorries waiting to unload outside the Chiu-Chow rice wholesaler, at the rubber trader next door to us the wife had taken over. She called the warehouse, she checked the quotes on futures, she bought and sold. To my father what went on at the rubber dealer was a wonder, executed with telephones and fax machines, involving huge turnovers he could only have dreamed about. In a sense, my father had felt he was in good company, that he too could make it rich, that he need not face the world with cringing unworthiness. He was sure he would not be left behind by the rice wholesalers and the rubber dealers. They had their near magical commodities, but he had his pearl, ginseng and antler velvet.

For the author of *Capital*, a commodity of capitalist production takes on fetishistic quality for the concealment of its social character. Capitalist commodity appears in an illusion of objective form in the marketplace—in the nature of 'existence of things qua commodity'. It is near magical, no labour power has made it, no power and ideology has helped to organize its production, it comes into existence by itself.[13] But we can also see such fetishism as a positive force, which a petite capitalist finds irresistible and proceeds to exploit it. This is a thinking of a different ideological hue. It comes to him as commercial opportunity, and as a means of redeeming his disadvantages and 'littleness'. The pearl-ginseng-deer antler trinity was the stuff of dreams and imaginations; they fed my father's mind and drove him.

Meanwhile, he persisted and consolidated his resources. A cautious man, he knew the pearl-ginseng-deer antler market was small and the pugnacious profit taking would not last. He had given up the medical consultation, and he did not want to shift from the core business of herbs and packaged remedies. He knew he would need to move on to the next venture though he did not know what it would be. But it had to be steadier than dealing with patent medicine and the precious pearl, ginseng and deer antler, and hopefully bringing in similar returns.

## Notes

1. Georg Simmel, *The Philosophy of Money*, David Frisby (ed.), London and NY: Routledge, 2005, p. 62.
2. James C. Scott, *Two Cheers for Anarchism*, Princeton: Princeton University Press, 2012, p. 112.
3. Raymond Williams, *Keywords*, NY: OUP, 1985, p. 46
4. Scott, *Two Cheers for Anarchism*, p. 85.
5. Alan and Josephine Smart (eds.), *Petty Capitalists and Globalization: flexibility, entrepreneurship, and economic development*, NY: SUNY Press, 2012, p. 2.
6. Ibid.
7. In Malaysia today, many of the Chinese healers are still self-taught. Some have attended Kuala Lumpur Academy of Traditional Chinese Medicine, and for those with funding the Beijing Chinese Medicine University, China, is the popular choice.
8. https://ctext.org/shang-han-lun/bian-mai-fa. Accessed 2 August, 2018.
9. My disclaim of expertise is no mere ritual of modesty. The exoteric and complex system of Chinese healing would test any interested layperson. At the same time, to speak of 'pharmacological properties' is to fit Chinese medicine into the Western scientific framework. Not surprisingly, the major complaint of Chinese medicine is that its efficacy cannot often be reproduced, and fails in the standardized guideline in gauging the cure of a specific remedy. See: Kecheng; Jia, Nati; Jiang, Nan; Wang, Feng; Kou, Junping, 'Beneficial effect of Danggui-Shaoyao-San, a traditional Chinese medicine, on drowsiness induced by chronic restraint stress', *Neuroscience Letters*, June 15, 2015, Vol. 597, pp. 26–31.
10. http://www.itmonline.org/arts/antler.htm. Accessed 7 August, 2018.

11. See my *The Malayan Emergency, Essays on a small and distant war*, Copenhagen: NIAS Press, 2016.
12. http://www.worldstopexports.com/malaysias-top-10-exports. Accessed 7 January, 2019.
13. Karl Marx, Capital, vol. 1 [1867]: translated by S. Moore and E. Aveling, in R.C. Tucker (ed), *The Marx-Engels Reader*, NY: W.W. Norton, 1978, pp. 319–329.

## Bibliography


Marx, Karl. 1978. 'Capital, vol. 1'. R. C. Tucker (ed), *Marx and Engels Reader.* NY: W.W. Norton, 319–29.

Scott, James C. 2012. *Two Cheers for Anarchism.* Princeton: Princeton University Press.

Simmel, Georg. 2005. *The Philosophy of Money.* David Frisby (ed), London and NY: Routledge.

Smart, Alan, and Josephine Smart. (eds.) 2012. *Petty Capitalists and Globalization.* Albany: SUNY Press.

Williams, Raymond. 1985. *Keywords.* NY: Oxford University Press.

Yao Souchou, 2016. *The Malayan Emergency: Essays on a Small, Distant War.* Copenhagen: NIAS Press.

Zhou, Kecheng, Nati Jia, Nan Jiang, Feng Wang, and Junping Kou. 2015. 'Beneficial Effect of Danggui-Shaoyao-San, a Traditional Chinese Medicine, on Drowsiness Induced by Chronic Restraint Stress', *Neuroscience Letters,* 597: 26–31.


### Internet Resources


Subhuti Dharmananda, 'Deer antler to Nourish Blood, Bone, and Joints', http://www.itmonline.org/arts/antler.htm. Accessed August 7, 2018.

Workman, Daniel, 'Malaysia's Top 10 Exports', http://www.worldstopexports.com/malaysias-top-10-exports. Accessed August 30, 2019.

CHAPTER 2

# The Shop on High Street

The Asian shophouse came out of the trade and commerce of the colonial era. After colonialism, in the post-war years, as cities were rebuilt, many thought it as an obstacle to urban development. Today, its fortunes have changed. The colonial shophouse is now celebrated as 'a continuity of the past, an old "way of life", [as] a purveyor of cultural-social mores, and a moral form of low energy (and slow) architecture against an age of conspicuous consumption and speed', an architectural historian has put it.[1] Tourists and heritage enthusiasts rave about the grand shophouses in Penang or Malacca or Singapore. These were elegant mansions built by wealthy Straits Chinese to settle their families, in a display of wealth and status. Nowadays these shophouses are much sought after by builders-investors who turn them into boutique hotels and guesthouses. The more modest shophouses are found in any city, in any small town. These are homespun and unremarkable, so common that you barely take notice of them as you walk along the street. But they make up their insignificance by their sheer ubiquity; they are everywhere, they define the city and the town. This is the world of petite capitalism—a profusion of premises in which merchants and tradesmen carry out their businesses and trades. And these shophouses have mostly stuck to their namesake: each is a place of work, and each is a place of living. This is true especially in the small towns—real estate prices have tended to forbid their residential use in the cities—where shophouses are run with the family working on the ground level and living upstairs. I grew up in


S. Yao, *The Shop on High Street*,
https://doi.org/10.1007/978-981-15-2031-0_2

one of the shophouses in Kuala Lumpur, and it is easy for me to detect in them a grandeur of form, a certain functional vitality.

Let us play the architect and take a closer look. Notice the façade of the neo-classical style that accentuating the clean planar surfaces? The frontage is free from projections which would have produced a myriad of shades and shadows, a compromise of the classical aesthetics.[2] Instead it appears as a smooth singular massing, and you can almost imagine the mock-Grecian columns designed to give the structure strength and dignity. But the reverie is but a fantasy. Classicism of the 1930s does not quite cut it, what grabs your attention is the tropical innovation. Looking at a row of colonial shophouses, you face a string of identical frontages of uniform façade. This is the five-foot path: a contiguous colonnaded, covered walkway. It forms a line of arcades that connect the shops, and before each shop it creates a moat of meagre space that separates each shop from the street. As the topography dictates, the five-foot path follows a straight line or it gently bends and curves as if in motion, taking the shophouses along with it. The five-foot path is nothing but functional. It protects the shops and the passers-by from the elements, it provides shelter for the loading and unloading of goods, and the shops take liberty by spilling their activities right to the kerb.

Each time I go back and seek out the old family shop, a rapt vision of these shophouses—a garland of unassuming buildings—takes up my mind. They are no longer familiar to me, as hyperinflation of real estate prices and urban development have produced different incarnations. From a Chinese medicine dealer, the shop on 53 High Street had morphed into a grocery, then a rice wholesaler and is now a boutique backpacker's hotel.

My daughter Neena and I go inside and find a seat in the café under a grand skylight. It's ten in the morning, and the café is so bright that it's as if the oppressive light has traced our footsteps and followed us inside. Our eyes adjust and catch the goings-on: the waiter guiding the customers through the local menu of hot, spicy offerings; the young French tourists, chatty as morning birds, waiting for the van to take them on a city tour; the glass-chrome reception desk staffed by exuberant, tight-skirted Tamil girls. Everything about the place is dissonant with its rustic origin in my memory. The bland functionality is gone. I struggle to 'see' the old fittings: the naked florescent light left on at daytime; the wall shelving fitted with glass doors; and far back submerged in dim light, the long iron-wood table where my father and I used to do the accounts. They have been replaced by the clammy fervour of global tourism.

We finish our drinks and walk out. The shop next door to us, I point out to Neena, used to be a rubber dealer, run by a grossly fat Mr Lim who, as though to accentuate his prosperous look, had chosen a wife of gaunt and emaciated frame; it is now a karaoke bar. The patchy, desolate feel of money and development prods us along. Further down the shoe store is still there. It no longer deals in gumboots and white canvas shoes, but fashionable leather footwear and joggers from China. High Street, now renamed Jalan Tun H.S. Lee after the country's first finance minister, holds its breath at another onslaught of developers and architects. Already the Hong Kong and Shanghai Bank building has taken over the square that used to be occupied by hawkers and food stalls. Where the street turns right before meeting the River Klang, the Public Islamic Bank, all glass and steel and 30-storeys high, with underground car park and indoor water-featured garden, points to the future. We gape at what remains of the shophouses, with their verandahs and five-foot paths and open monsoon drain by the kerb, each lost in the reverie of changes, counting its days...

The shop on 53 High Street had three floors. The shopfront took up the ground level, the warehouse the second floor and the third floor was the family living quarters. Space was at a premium, and so a new functional division was clumsily brokered. Typical of the neighbourhood shops, we ate in the kitchen with cartons of goods stacked by the doorway. Through the high school years I studied in the second-floor storeroom, where I read and did my homework next to cartons of May & Barker Cough Syrup piled high against the window. The third-floor living quarters, thanks to my mother, were clean and more or less free from clutter. Above it was the roof terrace. It was used for sun-drying the herbs and for hanging out the washing. At the corner we children made a garden with pots of chrysanthemums and evergreens, and next to it we installed a large fish tank from which fry and tadpoles would travel to their death in our school biology dissecting classes.

An ethnography of the colonial shophouse begins with the premises and the people who lived and worked there, but it should really start at the street and the neighbourhood. Thanks to the five-foot path, from the shop it was a few easy steps to the world outside.

Life at the shop began early in the kitchen. My mother got up at five in the morning, and stepped out to go to the Central Market a block away from the shop. At six-thirty we children got dressed and came downstairs to the kitchen. Mother had already been back, and the smell of rice porridge was strong and homely. Above the kitchen, the metal awning was half opened, and the light brushed the walls with an earth-yellow glow. Sitting at the table I heard from the back lane the cries of hawkers, the scuffle of feet on the gravel as people hurried to work.

Out in the street the morning light hit you in the face like a warning. The change of scene was sharp and blinding. One by one, the shops began to open. By the kerb in front of the shops, lorries were waiting to be unloaded, each expelling a cloud of diesel fume. The drivers watched nervously the traffic police, thinking: can this one be bribed, or maybe that one with a dark face and heavy moustache? The heat was rising. Your nose picked up the rancid odour of pickled radishes and salted fish, the sourness of dry rubber sheets. Your senses were alerted. And your eyes were open to the surrounding: the crows flying down from the electric wire to peck at the food scraps by the gutter; the hawkers and pedestrians emerging and filling the street; and in the far distance, the call for prayer from the old mosque by the river.

Writing about the shophouse makes one think of Bachelard's *Poetics of Space*.[3] It is impossible for anyone to have read the book and still see a building as mere bricks and mortar. The High Street shop was a place of buying and selling, but my mind is caught up with emotions and sensations more real to me than what went on at the shopfront. Bachelard has in mind the house or home, *la maison*, the symbol of the European bourgeoisie. *Poetics of Space* gives a powerful sense of home as place of intimacy, a place where we can think our thoughts and recollect our dreams, and perhaps discover something of ourselves.[4]

Let us follow Bachelard and take a philosopher's tour of the shophouse, our eyes missing nothing, our minds taking in each dent, each crevice, over the three floors.

The shophouse has no cellar, and the merging of work and living in a single place confuses things considerably. A cellar or a basement would have been a useful addition. Bachelard sees the cellar as source of psychic terror; to enter the place to immerse in its 'subterranean force', its 'primitivity' of one's fear.[5] If the High Street shop had a basement, we would have used it for storage. Or we could, in our widest fantasy, murder a creditor or two and bury the bodies there in the manner of the Gary Grant classic *Arsenic and Old Lace* (1946). The ground floor—not the cellar—is the root of the colonial shophouse. For Bachelard the ground level of the European house is mundane, uninteresting: a 'platitude of common life', he calls it.[6] For the shophouse the ground floor is everything. It is the shopfront. It is where trading and profit making take place. It is the reason for the shophouse's existence. If, following Bachelard, we see the colonial shophouse as an oneiric place sustained by dreams and imagination, then the hopes and the promiscuous optimism of the petite capitalist are rooted here at the ground floor.

The second floor is relatively banal. It is the storage area. The stairs creak as you ascend the stairs, and through the gloom your eyes barely make out the sacks of herbs, the cartons of milk powder tins stacked high, the boxes of dried lizards and shrivelled toads on bamboo sticks. Your eyes settle, and you notice the shopboys have squeezed a corner out of the clutter for their own use. There they have put a small table where they read and write letters. Next to it, on the wall, they have hung a mirror under a naked light bulb, before which they learn to dance to Abba—*Waterloo* is their favourite—from a cassette player. And further on, a space has been cleared so that Ah Khaw the amateur musician can practise his harmonica. You envy the shopboys' ingenuity, their ability to carve out of the dusty chaos a space of their own you didn't think possible.

You want to stay a bit, but it is working hours. People are coming and going, retrieving a carton here and carrying away a bale of poppy husks there. You climb the stairs and reach the third floor, and everything signals the home proper. It is a place of rest; it offers a respite from what goes on at the ground floor. Here our parents talk and relaxed and listen to the music that seemed to unite them in marriage: recordings of Peking opera by the diva Mei Lanfang. Here in our bedrooms we read and study and do our homework, and get an update on the Top 20s from the radio. Here our parents receive their guests, the conversations taken up matters that my father, as chairman of the Dabu Hakka Association, would need to attend to. There is hard talk too of money and business matters, which drifts to our rooms with their complicated urgency. But they always hold back, and the conversation soon returns to more congenial subjects: the weddings they plan to attend, the donations to schools they have been asked to give, the welfare of their families. There are social visits and laughter and simple domestic pleasures at the third-floor living quarters. Only the armchair where my father takes his daily insulin shots augurs grave, melancholic things.

Bachelard describes the bourgeoise home as a place of reveries.

> I should say: the house shelters day-dreaming, the house protects the dreamer, the house allows one to dream in peace. ... We comfort ourselves by reliving memories of protection. Something closed must retain our

> memories, while leaving them their original value as images. Memories of the outside world will never have the same tonality as those of home ...[7]

The home allows memory to do its work, to recreate the past and the external world with its 'tonality' so different from that of the home. It is the same with the shophouse. We who lived in it felt safe and protected. And as though taking hint from the philosopher of space, we had turned the shophouse into a place that gave licence to dream, to fantasize, to add our experiences to the store of recollections. And I think of the living quarters at the third floor: it was a place of rest that sealed off the busy world downstairs. The ground floor and the living quarters are allocated their contrasting functions: one of work, one of rest and where one dreams of escape.

A house, Bachelard writes, 'shelters day-dreaming', 'protects the dreamer', 'and allows one to dream in peace'.[8] *Poetics of Space* has a view that the house is a place of solitude that cuts one off from the intrusions of a corrupting world: a distinctively modern thought. And how easily is this sanctuary of rest and dreams invaded!

For all the nostalgic yearning, when I think of the shophouse I think of as well the chaos and the state of disarray. It is almost as though the original architect had aimed to make the place a tad unliveable. The third floor was an exception only because it was the living quarters. It is not too much to say that the colonial shophouse had been designed with the petite capitalist and his needs in mind. Putting the family and business under one roof has a touch of genius: it enforces supreme practicality and it merges working and living in a single space. The shophouse saves costs. At the High Street shop, there was no separate budget for the family and for the shop's maintenance. There was a single electric meter, and since the workers ate with us in the shop, all the food costs were put under a single account. At the same time, living where we worked enabled us to serve the customers at all hours. A man would come and knock at the door at two in the morning and asked for a bottle of Panadol Suspension for a sick child. You couldn't turn him away. You treated it like a mercy mission, and besides it created goodwill and helped to build the customer base.

There were other examples of the shophouse's practicality, but nothing can compare with the values and ethos it—the architectural form itself—so powerfully shaped and nurtured.

With my parents, the petite capitalist ethos was full of the ideas sacrifice and collective labour. It was a kind of joyful self-enslavement.

Whether the original architect had this in mind or not, the design felt like aiming to spur its residents to work and be productive, and domestic enjoyment was a reward for the deserving.

In his memoir *Father and Son*, the Victorian writer Edmund Gosse writes about his own birth:

> [For my parents] pleasure was found nowhere but in the Word of God, and to the endless discussion of the Scripture when the day's work was done.To this strange household the event of a child was not welcome but born with resignation. The event was thus recorded in my Father's diary: "E. delivered a son. Received green swallow from Jamaica." (Gosse senior was a naturalist and author.)[9]

It was a remarkable lapse in protocol. Putting work before the birth of his son painted a sad, dismal picture of the father. Gosse doesn't think so. His father was only being 'scrupulous'.

> This entry has caused amusement, as showing that he was as much interested in the bird as in the boy. But this does not follow; what the wording exemplifies is my Father's extreme punctilio. The green swallow arrived later in the day than the son, and the earlier visitor was therefore recorded first; my Father was scrupulous in every species of arrangement.[10]

The diary entry gives note to his parents' religious devotion, to their austere homely pleasures. And it describes his father's sense of order. He was being methodical: the bird arrived first, the son's birth later, so it was recorded accordingly. Yet you can't help feeling that to Gosse, the curt announcement of the two 'deliveries', one of life, one of dead biological specimen, made a certain point. The father was busy with his writing and his scientific investigation, and he was one with his wife in their devotion to the Scripture. There was no idleness in the Gosse household. Perhaps it says something of the Gosse senior's personal character—that being busy justifies most things, and meaningful labour demands sacrifice. The virtue of work, not the lapse in protocol, was the explanation of the father's endearing absent mindedness.

If my father had committed a similar act of folly, it would have been told and retold until it settled into a family legend. Nonetheless my father was punctilious, not unlike Gosse senior. My father was not Christian; he was ignorant of the Bible. But he was, in his fashion, given to sermonizing about the importance of work and virtue. Instead of the Script, he had his parables. He was fond of the age-old 'The Foolish Old Man Who Moved Mountains'. His face lit up when he told it, and as he came to the old man's punchline: 'My children, my grandchildren, my great-grandchildren will finish the task after I am gone', he raised his fisted hand for emphasis. 'They will go on but the mountains won't grow taller!' His exegesis piled one notion on top of another, until it reached the zenith of an idea: the idea of resilience and strength of character across generations.

My father's approach to personal character is the phrase 'to be a person', xou jen. For him there is not greater shame than to be accused of 'no knowing how to be a person', a familiar social censure of Confucian philosophy. And this shamefulness covers bad deeds and bad thought. As he often put it: Think before you say something; words can hurt people. Xou is the word for making in the transitive sense, but also, more interestingly, denotes a state of thought, a state of being. The Confucian inferences are perhaps too extravagant. What my father had in mind was a kind of moral democracy: anyone can have a go at being good.

Each time I think about the shophouse, comes to mind how we worked and worked together. It seems to me the best expression of what my father had in mind about being good. As children we put our juvenile needs aside and did our share of the chores. We all helped in the shop, we ran little errands, we picked up packages too small to be delivered, I helped with the accounts. In a shophouse, work and family life were intimately merged. There was tedium, but there was also happy collective labour. Sometimes the idea of home and the way we worked reached a pitch of perfection that the recollection makes me dizzy with yearning.

It had been the practice of the Chinese herbalist shop to manufacture humdrum medicines like skin lotion, medical oil, and heat-reducing drinks. These were easy to make, based on simple formulas and using common ingredients. Often, they were manufactured in a kitchen or in a workshop, and they were popular and sold well. Even today a taxi driver would, after a day's shift, drop by at a shop and pick up a bottle of Rhinoceros Water, a cooling agent allegedly containing horn shavings of the animal in near extinction. There is Sea Coconut Cough Syrup, its main ingredient said to be palm coconut from Seychelles in East Africa; it brings relief from dry, chesty cough—a sign of over-heating of the lungs. The most famous of the home-made remedies is the legendary Tiger Balm. Tiger Balm was invented by a herbalist and his two sons the Aw brothers in British Burma in the late 1880s. They saw a market for an all-rounded medical rub and proceeded to bring out an oil-based balm that guaranteed relief from rheumatism to headache, from muscle strain to insect bites. Tiger Balm is now a multinational brand sold throughout Asia and many parts of the world and manufactured in factories in Singapore, China, India (Hyderabad) and Thailand.

Tiger Balm was already a best seller in my father's time of the seventies. It had a near monopoly of the rubbing balm market, but it enriched the manufacturer and wholesalers, leaving very little for the retail shops, as my father liked to complain. He was not happy with the tiny profit margin he earned from a dozen or a gross of the product. So the venture to take on Tiger Balm was part commercial avarice, part daring to see if he could cut a slice of its enormous market.

My father was fond of such home industry projects. When he wanted to try out an idea, we all had to live through weeks of product testing. One of his inventions was toothpowder, which he hoped would replace the Colgate toothpaste we normally used. For a time, a small dish of grey powder sat on the sink next to the tap, and each day we would dip our toothbrushes into the watery mess and run it through our teeth. We wanted to support the inventor, but the toothpowder was gritty and flavourless, tasting like uncooked batter. We persisted, but the novelty soon ran out. The toothpowder was left on the sink untouched, then my mother, sensing her husband's defeat, tactfully removed it from the bathroom.

The Twin-Heart Medical Balm was a different kind of project. It had commercial prospects, and it was to be a family undertaking. To take on the most famous over-the-counter Chinese medicine: the idea was bold and promising.

We started with choosing a brand name. The children put in their bid. We agreed the brand had to sound modern; it had to avoid the impression of riding on the coattails of Tiger Balm. But none of the suggestions felt right. Monkey Balm felt too close to Tiger Balm; Pink Baby Balm second sister preferred was too cute, suggesting its use only for young infants. Twin-Heart was an idea I took from a book on Greek mythology I had read at the British Council library. Cupid's arrowing piercing two hearts had a sense of foreign associations, modern and mysterious. So Twin-Heart Balm it was. We didn't want to ape the competitor, but we hoped Cupid's arrow as a trademark would be as memorable as the ferocious beast in Asia.

In my father's generation there was a bible of home industry that had inspired—and frustrated—many schemes of domestic manufacturing. *Qong Shan Quan Shu*, Encyclopaedia of Industrial and Commercial Sciences, was first published in 1935 by The Commercial Press in Shanghai. A copy of the 1961 edition I inherited listed the main ingredients of medical balm: camphor, menthol, cajuput oil, mint oil and clove oil. They work to open up the pores and penetrate muscles. We would, like Tiger Balm, make a red version by adding cassia oil—to appease Muslim users who were given to suspect white medical balm contained pork lard.

Once we had decided on the brand name and the labelling, we picked an evening for making our Twin-Heart Medical Balm. In a sly homage to the more famous brand, we called it the Tiger Balm evening. On such an occasion, our parents, us children, all gathered at the kitchen—no one was left out.

Father had already prepared the mixture of the ingredients in a stainless-steel pot. It now sat over the stove and slowly simmering.

We watched the thick white vapour rising, sensing the sting on our nostrils. Father set his feet before the stove, and as though a gesture of self-sacrifice, stared down at the concoction and stirred it with a long wooden ladle. Meanwhile we children washed the small glass bottles and wiped them dry, and mother began putting them to steam in a large wok. 'Are the bottles ready? It will be about ten minutes', father turned his head and said. They were ready: the first batch of glass bottles, five dozens exactly, having been steamed and sterilized, rested on the bamboo tray. The home chemist, wearing a pair of rubber gloves and with a spoon, began to dish out a measure of the molten balm in each bottle. It was delicate work, but he made barely a spillage. We too were quietly efficient. We wiped the rim of each bottle, then screwed on the cap. Mother and second sister, their hands clean and dry, came and took the tray and glued on the labels. We did this, when finished started another round of bottling and capping and putting on the labels. It was a messy nostril-stinging work, but oddly satisfying.

The work was done and we took turns to wash at the sink. We were careful, as a smear of the eye would cause sting and havoc. I stood by my father and dripped turpentine onto his hands. He rubbed rigorously; his face had the distant look of one who has worked hard. He finished it off with a generous application of soap. Then it was my turn, with him pouring turpentine on my hands. We wiped our hands and turned to look at what we had achieved: from the table the bottles were like rows of wooden toy soldiers, assembled and varnished by a hobbyist's loving hands.

We did this once in a couple of months. As I look back, it seems so much had happened in those evenings. We were a team; we all took pleasure in each other's company. Mother, at times harsh with her children, was in a good mood. And father, having made himself the team leader, was full of confidence and commitment to his latest venture. These were the golden hours of peace and grace I did not often experience in the shop.

Twin-Heart Balm never made the money we had hoped. We had invested little, and labour was free, so we didn't lose much. Nonetheless it appeared to have made a modest entry in the night markets and the village shops. After the High Street shop's closing, the patent of Twin-Heart Medical Balm was given to one of our ex-workers who ran a shop in Kajang. Ah Loong had been one the shopboys sent to us by their parents, and he had stayed on and learned the herbal business. So giving him the patent was the right thing to do. I had in mind that it would reward his loyalty, and besides Twin-Heart Balm needed a custodian and found one.

When he came to the shop, we had talked and I congratulated him for having his own shop. We were of the same age, and we had been close when he was staying with us. I asked him how he would go about making the balm. 'I took a peek at how your family did it in the kitchen', he said. 'I'll just follow what you did.' He was pleased as hell when he said it. The family had engaged in industrial theft, and he was to follow suit. Our family's larceny was ambitious as his was modest. He deserved the limited prosperity Twin-Heart might deliver, I thought. I helped him to load the couple of cartons of Twin-Heart Balm left in the storeroom onto his van, adding the fridge and the cane chairs no longer needed. I said goodbye and stood at the verandah and watched him drive off.

A few years back, in 2015, I was at a village in Southern Thailand researching for a book. It was Peace Village No. 10, where some of the ex-Malayan communist insurgents had settled after the signing of the 1989 peace accord between the communists and the Malaysian and Thai governments.[11] At a ramshackle provision shop, Twin-Heart Balm stared back at me from the grimy shelf of undressed timber. I had gone in for a bottle of mineral water. I looked around and the shop owner eyed at me encouragingly: 'Buy something, anything'. His wife was urging her child in a baby walker to take another spoonful of mush, and there was the general clutter of disposal nappies and laundry detergent and brooms and plastic buckets. Mostly my eyes were caught by the home brand medical balm of my childhood. It was a long time since I saw a bottle; the balm has survived; it has lived on. In Ah Loong's capable hands, it has somehow spread to as far as southern Thailand. The veil of years and distance was lifted. I sat by the counter and drank my mineral water. I didn't want to leave. The child, as though to escape its mother, forced the baby walker inside the shop and for a moment lost in the dark. My eyes followed him, and from the dark at the back of the shop—that must be the kitchen—came my father's voice: 'Come on, it's the last batch. Let's finish the job!' I was startled by the familiar urgency. I wanted to rush into the kitchen, to that voice, and cry out, 'I am sorry I am late. Wait for me. Don't leave me out!' For a few moments, it all came back to me—the happiness, the joyful labour, the family romance.

I left and calmed down. As I reached the hostel my thoughts had settled. And I asked myself the question as I do now: where did my parents' values and sense of virtue come from?

When I think about it, everything about my parents comes across as a patchwork of negotiated relationships and cultural fragments. When I say my father was conservative in his way, I want to add that he read modern literature and favoured his daughters over his sons. My mother was loyal to her husband, but she was given to arguing with him and questioning his decisions. And my father's sense of 'what is done is done' resignation is an echo of Daoism or even of the ideas of Daoist philosopher Zhuangzi whose work he read. As for the virtue of work much is directed to the family and its welfare. The family justifies everything, and the family happiness and prosperity warrant the best of one's efforts and sacrifices. When this is elevated to the realm of cultural ideology, family labour becomes near sacred. And as a cultural ideal, there is nothing more inviolable than the idea of a family working and striving together. Here labour needs no justification and even pecuniary return seems secondary in importance.

And here, if I were having a discourse with my parents, the ancestors and their blessings would make their way into the conversation.

My parents were not devout worshippers. My mother was quick to dismiss the wives of family friends who went to Penang, to Bangkok, searching for temples to pray at—spiritual shopping trips for the idle rich. Religious worship should be sensible and moderate. There is public worshiping, of course, when a deity's birthday is celebrated by the whole community. But many seasonal rituals can be done at home. During the Hungry Ghost Festival—the Chinese All Souls Day—we went to the cemetery and made offering to our grandparents' grave, but a more intimate affair took place at home ending with a dinner that felt like a reward for piety. Ritual carried out at home gives the home a spiritual identity, making it the focus of the blessings of gods and deities. My grandmother said: to burn incense at the altar is to show the gods the way to come, that we are pious and we remember them.

In the family, during any seasonal festival the kitchen god was never forgotten. The worship of any deities ended up with prayers and ritual offerings before the kitchen god as though he was the leader of the pantheon. The altar was sited high next to the stove. It was a composite of altars: kitchen good sitting next to Guanyin, the goddess of mercy, Kuan Ti, the god of commerce and loyalty, the ancestors whose wooden tablet was mark: 'The Honourable Seat of the Yao Forefathers'. In the Chinese cosmology, the spiritual realm is a mirror of the secular world; one is a faithful reflection of the other.[12] To worship the deities is to fulfil their wish to be remembered by the living, in the way those living want their existence to be acknowledged. We treat our ancestors with respect, approbation and honour, and these are the same standards with which we conduct ourselves in *this* world. And just as we love others and fear those who have power over us, we, too, love and fear our ancestors. The principle is: an ancestor remembered by the living becomes a deity and lives in heaven; an ancestor neglected turns rouge into a ghost out to haunt and harm the living. Ancestral worship is glossed with fear, as much as with love and reverence.

Domestic rituals and worship mattered to us because we were not church goers. Chinese family business was for us a world of tradition, with a more or less defined ethnic character. Each shophouse was, almost as a rule, marked by the kitchen god inside, and the earth god outside before the door way at the five-foot path. They were sites of the spirits, yet more than that. They joined the present with the past, the cloudy realm of ancient tradition with the hurly burly of everyday life. The spirits and deities, their blessings and warnings, were brought down to earth, so to speak. Their significance and efficacies were hard to ignore; they ruled our lives and shaped the fortune of the shop. And daily reminders of the good works of the ancestors made sure we children got the message. When I received a good grade in school, when I won the first prize of Junior Interschool Calligraphy Competition, the lesson was: see, how the ancestors have blessed you—for being good, for remembering to burn incense at their altars. There was no talk of my practices, no recognition of my determination to make a grab for personal glory. There was insistent coaxing of certain values. Reward and punishment would be meted out by beings beyond this world. Since both thinking and conduct are social acts, one is responsible for them as for any kind of social act. Ancestral worship brings thought and conduct into a single realm of significance. It helps us to achieve the 'sensitivity to the Good' that defines one's virtue and moral goodness.[13]

My parents' idea of virtue was homebound and involved devotion to work—as endorsed by the gods and ancestors. But the work we did had a context; the family labour took place in a colonial shophouse. Its built form and aesthetics affected much of the ways we worked: a bit of architectural determinism is not out of place here.

It seems innocuous enough. The word shophouse has since the colonial days written without a hyphen. The linguistic slip fuses the two basics of life that affect most people: work and domestic arrangement. Shophouse is like the word livelihood—both denote the two functions: living and working. Whether or not the designer had this in mind, the fact is the petite capitalist enterprise cannot be run like a nine-to-five job of a suburban dweller. For a shopkeeper like my father, it would be a betrayal of good sense if he was to live elsewhere and travel to work each day—even if he could afford to have a house elsewhere. The contemporary term for working from home is telecommuting. It often touted as convenient and saving transport costs, and a mother can work in the home office—often the kitchen table—while looking after her young infant. But working from home is isolating, and denies homeworkers the social contact and the pleasure of gossip over the water fountain. For most, the blurring of the two regions of work and home is not a happy experience.

Whether or not the designer had this in mind, the shophouse brokers this clumsy marriage of home life and work life. The built form articulates the singular truth that a petite capitalist enterprise cannot be run like a nine-to-five job of a suburban dweller. We in the family had at times found living in the shophouse oppressive; there was no escape from work. Like the contemporary telecommuter, we wanted less the domination of work that encroached on us like a never ending vendetta. The shopkeeper has to live in the shop because he is the anchor, his presence the sign of its reputation and prosperity. Everything about the shophouse is a cue to the cultural logic: work is living, and living takes its significance from work. It says: petite capitalists are no layabouts, and they look after their families.

Buying and selling take place within the shophouse, but the premises are also a place for the making of culture. Bachelard's effusive reading of the bourgeoise home points to the private reverie and modern yearnings that it nurtures. The architectural form matters. So it is with the colonial shophouse. Chinese petite capitalism thrives on economic pressures and social values about work and its values. But it appears to me that each business premises is a glasshouse, where certain values and ethos are carefully brought to bloom like rare orchards. A shophouse is as nothing if it does not manufacture the work ethics so crucial to the working of petite capitalism.

With Chinese petite capitalism, the idea of work is more than what it says. There is the grinding of the machine and sweatshop servitude in its connotations. Family labour is a special kind of labour. When family members are also the workers, when family relationships are the means of organizing work and distributing the surpluses, there is perfect unity in the activities important to every family business. But then, when capital ownership and labour are the family itself, the production is significantly skewed. Harshness on the shop floor and the relentless goading of the family are muted because these are for the collective good, because they contribute to the family's prosperity. However which way we look at it, the term exploitation won't do, not even the clumsy 'self-exploitation'.[14] There is a gender aspect to this, of course. Women—and the young—are often exploited in an enterprise controlled by men. Yet it would rash to think that family and marriage do not create a ground for cooperation, and make sharing of work and profit almost natural and frictionless. In each shophouse, the family labour is, as they say, a labour of love. Is that why in the family labour is often elevated as virtue?

So we are back where we've started. In a way we can look at the shophouse as figured by a powerful ideology. Its wondrous architectural features, its heritage values, its 'slow' built form in a fast urban setting: it is easy to forget a family lives there, a type of productive activity and labour relations take place within it. When profit making is full of the talk of virtue and personal character, it comes across as a perverse gesture. More suitably, you can look at Chinese petite capitalism as a beast at once savage and at peace, a form of economic production where harsh labour conditions and the ethos of sharing—of work and profit—are both prominent features. Yet it is also true that the passion of petite capitalism is mercenary, a fact that causes those working in a shophouse a lot of grief and hardship. The idea of virtue and moral conduct shades over the calculations and tough decisions. In a family business, those disadvantaged cannot be so indelicate as to care for only profit and money. Production is one thing, and the shophouse always points a finger at the happier side of things: the joyful collective labour, the cooperation with friends and kin, the fair treatment of ones we deal with. These values and realities were a panacea for the materialist bent of family-based production. For the petite capitalist, there's also a lot to be said for not being too virtuous, for not being too much of a good person.

## Notes

1. Wong Yunn Chii and Johannes Widodo (eds), *Shophouse/townhouse: Asian perspectives.* Singapore: Department of Architecture, School of Design & Environment, National University of Singapore, 2016, p. 1. I am grateful to Professor Lilian Chee for sending me the book.
2. Hong Weng Hin and others (eds), *Encounters With Ipoh: Familiar landscape, untold stories.* Singapore: CASA, Dept of Architecture, NUS and KL: CORE, Faculty of Built Environment, University of Malaya, 2013, pp. 26–29.
3. Gaston Bachelard, *The Poetics of Space*: trans. Maria Jolas, Boston: Beacon Press, 1969.
4. This has an echo in Virginia Woolf's essay *A Room of One's Own* which has a clear feminist slant. Virginia Woolf, *A Room of One's Own*, London: Hogarth Press, 1929.
5. Gaston Bachelard, *The Poetics of Space*, pp. 18–19.
6. Ibid., p. 110.
7. Ibid., p. 6.
8. Ibid., p. 6.
9. Edmond Goose, *Father and Son: A study of two temperaments*, London: William Heinemann, 1909, p. 6.
10. Ibid.
11. See my *The Malayan Emergency, Essays on a small distant war*, Copenhagen: NIAS Press, 2016.
12. See Stephen Feuchtwang, 'Domestic and communal worship in Taiwan'. In *Religion and Ritual in Chinese Society*, Arthur Wolf (ed), Stanford: Stanford University Press, 1974, pp. 105–29.
13. Clifford Geertz, *Available Light: Anthropological reflections on philosophic topics*, Princeton: Princeton University Press, 2002, p. 22.
14. Alan Smart and Josephine Smart (eds), *Petty capitalists and globalization: Flexibility, entrepreneurship, and economic development.* Albany: SUNY Press, 2005, p. 6.

## Bibliography

Bachelard, Gaston. 1969. *The Poetics of Space*. Boston: Beacon Press.

Feuchtwang, Stephen. 1974. 'Domestic and communal worship in Taiwan', in *Religion and Ritual in Chinese Society*, Arthur Wolf (ed.), Stanford: Stanford University Press, pp. 105–130.

Geertz, Clifford. 2002. *Available Light: Anthropological Reflections on Philosophic Topics*. Princeton: Princeton University Press.

Gosse, Edmund. 1909. *Father and Son*. London: William Heinemann.

Hong, Weng Hin and others. (eds). 2013. *Encounters With Ipoh: Familiar Landscape, Untold Stories*. Singapore: CASA, Dept of Architecture, NUS and KL: CORE, Faculty of Built Environment, University of Malaya.

Scott, James C. 2012. *Two Cheers for Anarchism*. Princeton: Princeton University Press.

Smart, Alan, and Josephine Smart. (eds). 2012. *Petty Capitalists and Globalization*. Albany: SUNY Press.

Williams, Raymond. 1985. *Keywords*. NY: Oxford University Press.

Wong, Yunn Chii, and Johannes Widodo (eds). 2015. *Shophouse/Townhouse: Asian Perspectives*. Singapore: Department of Architecture, NUS.

Woolf, Virginia. 1929. *Room of One's Own*. London: Hogarth Press.

Yao, Souchou. 2016. *The Malayan Emergency: Essays on a small, distant war*. Copenhagen: NIAS Press.

CHAPTER 3

# 'She's Not Your Kin, But She Is Your Aunt'

My father was always busy, and he seemed to give himself over to so many community duties, so many business meetings and dinners that he had little time for his family. And my mother often complained: why waste time on all the socializing that brought nothing but grovellers and sly favour-seekers? But then these duties and meeting and dinners were his world. This was where he got the latest pricing on certain goods, where he found out about the bargains to be had with one wholesaler versus another, the news of opening of new shops in the neighbourhood—quite apart the pleasure of seeing his friends. In *The Great Transformation*, Karl Polanyi speaks of the embeddedness of the economy in social relationships and institutions in the modern society.[1] He was sceptical about Adam Smith's 'economic man' driven by self-interest, and he believed that 'man's economy, as a rule, is submerged in his social relationships.'[2] Social life and cultural values affect the way we manage our economic activities; the two spheres are intimately linked. The idea, not in so many words, was familiar to us at the High Street shop. My mother complained about it, we children lived with it, my father dug deep into it and made it the way to run his business.

My father liked to say, 'At home you rely on the family; out in the world you rely on your friends.' Included in 'friends' were relatives, kinfolk who are not your immediate family; so what he meant was 'out in the world you rely on your friends and kin.' The maxim has an unmistakable materialist ring. To tie social relationship with economic usefulness is so pervasive that the Chinese even have a word for it. Guanxi is a cultural ideal; it


S. Yao, *The Shop on High Street*,
https://doi.org/10.1007/978-981-15-2031-0_3

refers to economic transaction of a special sort. In economic text books, the market is full of competition, profit maximization, and the 'more for me and less for you' combativeness. Guanxi defies all this; to the Chinese petite capitalists the word—literally, relationship or social connection—is near magical. With a guanxi relationship making profit and making—and keeping—friends are possible. There is no contradiction in making money with/from friends. Between people so closely connected mistakes and bad feelings are easily amended and forgiven, and competitive violence quickly gives way to consensus and harmony. That's the theory anyhow: guanxi makes sure there is no conflict, no moral crisis, in the perfect merging of friendship and business dealing.

For someone like my father, the beauty of the guanxi idea is that all social relationships are potentially useful—like the thinking of an Amway franchisee. School and university mates, old co-workers, friends you made in a tour group or a dinner party can all be profitably exploited. Against my mother's apparent cynicism, my father would stick to his belief that time spent in guanxi building is time well spent. Time consuming, but it was livelihood. Yet we may ask: What does a petite capitalist really want out of the social relationships that make up his world? Is guanxi only about furtive self-interest in the guise of friendship? Against these questions, guanxi looks increasingly like an impossible idea. The fact is guanxi-based transactions work just as often as they do not. But that is nothing compared with its appeal, its promise of happy compromises. As with all human affairs, guanxi encompasses bad faith and betrayal and contestations. This is a story of small Chinese family business we often neglect to tell.

We called him Iron Monger Lee. Perhaps he had once been an ironsmith, or more likely, it was his dark, dusty face and stout bodily frame that gave him his name. His Abundant Prosperity Medicine Shop sat on the main street of Sungei Buloh township, in the outskirts of Kuala Lumpur. We arrived around three in the afternoon, feeling hot and sultry after the long drive. But we soon settled down at the shop, consoled by the familiar scene: the confusion of cartons and packages, the herbs and patent medicine, and from the shopfront the plastic buckets, brooms, Surf detergent, toilet rolls, disposable diapers that spilled onto the verandah. It looked busy and thriving, customers were being served at the counter and more were milling around. Manning the counter were Lee's elder son and his wife, while Mrs Lee pottered about at the back of the shop. Letting them take charge, Iron Monger Lee sat on the cane chair at the shopfront to take in the traffic and flows of passers-by. He gave the impression that Abundant Prosperity was a retirement project, and perhaps it was. In his fifties he was too young to be retired, but here he was, whiling away the time as if a well-deserved reward after a lifetime of working.

Our hosts urged us towards a low table by the counter, where they had laid out bottles of Coke, some Dutch biscuits and a pot of Oolong tea. Mrs Lee mumbled a few words and left us. I had accompanied my father on his trips to Sungei Buloh before and knew Lee's grumpy, rough-and-ready manners. He waved his hand over the table to get us sit down; he was polite but he made no fuss over his guests. A faint indifference sat on his face, as though he felt patronized by the visit of the city folk.

Before the two men began to talk, I readied myself for the ritual I knew was sure to come. I tensed up my body and Lee turned his eyes to me and said: Still the skinny boy, did you do the exercise I taught you? But he didn't wait for me to show him. You've got to do the exercise, he said. Come on, let me show you how Bruce Lee did it. He raised his fists, bent his legs and lowered his buttock into a half squat. Come on, push me hard. I pushed him hard on his chest. He was poised in the 'horse-shitting stance' of Shaolin kung fu, as he called it. He stood firm; he would not be moved. It happened every time we came for a visit. I took it as a kind of show-off, a kind of boasting. But of what? Virility maybe, or perhaps his need for one-upmanship in every social situation he found himself in.

My father watched indulgently. Lee was showing off, and I had strung along. I had the instinct my father had wanted me to go along with the horseplay, and recognized my meek attempt at helping him with the proceedings that would follow.

Lee and my father were old acquaintances. They had known each other through the many events of the Dabu Hakka Association. Lee was known for his gruff churlish manner, but he could be generous and big-hearted when these were expected of him. At the annual fundraising dinner, he was the first one to raise his hand to bid for the bottle of cognac, or the box of cigars, or the Seiko watch that had been put on auction. Some said Lee was just a bit too quick, just a bit too pugnacious with his bid. The fund raising should be a polite affair, they said, not an all-out competition for face and status. Still they were pragmatic folk. They all thought Lee, free with his purse, deserved his public gesture and the praise that went with it. And Lee and his wife were in it together. She was vivacious and full of talk, and she would goad her husband along: Make another bid. Go on. But then she's a Cantonese, spending money—and getting her husband to do so—came naturally to her. People liked to gossip, but Lee was unfailing in making his wife happy.

When the Lees started Abundant Prosperity, my father had helped them to draw up a list of goods to stock the shelves. He also advised them on the display: the old stock at the front, the fresh ones at the back. Lee was one of the amateur healers my father disproved of. Nonetheless he had coached him, passing over some of the books and pamphlets he no longer had the use for. Abundant Prosperity began to find its own way, and we continued to supply it and fill the orders. But Lee was not a man easy to deal with. As he said, I owe no one favours. There would be an argument each time a delivery had been made. The prices were not right, the ordered wrongly filled, the goods were not packed securely, Lee would complain. After one of Lee's exasperating phone calls, my father said: only those with money could be so tight-fisted. In his mind, Lee was two-faced and a grouchy bargain hunter, his jolly mien a disguise. After the phone call, my father would go and to sort things out, to smooth the temper. Often I was asked to tag along.

And out of frustration, during the drive, my father would reach out for the old tale. The tale about Lee's 'ill-gained wealth' had been circulating around for a while. When in his twenties, it was said, Lee was a leader of a criminal gang in Sungei Buloh that collected protection money from the bars and massage parlours, wisely avoiding the law-abiding retail shops. There were fights, there were beating up of clientele who had mistreated one of the girls, there were knife-out threats to bar owners who refused to pay up. Lee took the gang through the risky ventures until the police came and shut it down. Lee was lucky to avoid court charges and imprisonment. After that, he turned to traffic smuggled goods across the Thai-Malaysian border—diesel (then subsidized by the Malaysia government) to the north, cigarettes and liquor down to the south. He must have started Ever Prosperity to park his black money, my father would conclude.

The rumour mongering, for that's what it, was unworthy of my father, I thought. What happened to his 'never speak ill of people' approach to social relationship? It was for me a moment of loss of innocence—not only about my father, but also the duplicity of the adult world.

At the shop at Sungei Buloh, Lee's past was like the prelude to the staging of a business transaction. My father had once again come to ask his friend for a loan. You thought they had got their guanxi all worked out, but as it turned out, their financial dealing was messy and complicated.

We had finished our drinks and we were done with Lee's kung fu demonstration. We began to move to Lee's small office at the back. I picked up my steps and followed them. In the office Lee parked himself behind the desk, while we sat on the chairs before him. Lee's backslapping cheeriness had gone; he swirled his chair and tilted his eyes towards the window, while my father's face turned grave and anxious.

The asking came direct and matter-of-factly: I want to ask you for 3,000 ringgit. That is all I need. You have always come good; I hope you can this time.

Lee lowered his head and looked at his friend: I have some money coming, near 3000, someone owes me. I can let you have it.

He too was brisk and formal, his voice a touch of testiness. You know business is bad and it's hard for everyone, he said, but let us see if we can clear up the last loan.

My father turned to me, his eyes saying: Don't worry. Everything'll be alright. He reached his hand into the briefcase and took out the cheque.

Yes, business has been tough for everyone, he said. What I have in mind is to pay back the loan over three months, I can manage that. We can stick the same interest rate as before, if you agree …

I didn't like to see my father this way. It distressed me to see him having to deal with a person like Lee—the ex-gangster, the rustic tough money lender. The need for money had reduced my father to undignified abasement. I left them to their dealing and went for a walk around the block.

In the family we were accustomed to taking many things for granted. The High Street shop that fed and clothed us; its financial return that was the ground of our security; the prospect of a university education if we performed well in school—everything was hard-earned and bolstered by a good deal of hope. We were cocooned in our own prodigious optimism. As we got older, though, we were gradually hauled into the stress and anxiety of the family business. The Sungei Buloh visit had been one of those moments that revealed the blemishes of our existence. We worked hard and saved hard and we would dream and scheme, but we couldn't do without the help of others. We prized hard work and independence, but our life was tied to the decisions and generosity of other people. My father had asked Lee for a loan, and Lee had come good. Yet I couldn't help thinking that father as a prey to his friend's boorish manoeuvres.

We drove back to the city in the evening's last light. We reached the highway and it was a long stretch of traffic at the tolls. Inside the car Lee's cheque was safely in the briefcase, but we felt no triumph, no 'mission accomplished' satisfaction. For all his homily about guanxi and the sanctity of friendship and business connections, my father looked defeated. His high regard for the Chinese art of commerce felt to him like a sorry passion. Doing business with friends is culturally sensible, but it can be risky and socially ruinous.

As I call up that afternoon at Sungei Buloh, I feel again the sadness. A part of it was my sense of filial loyalty. I had the idea that going with my father was to share his burden, to make things easier for him. Now older and more objective, I ask myself: What is the problem here? He had gone out to get a loan, and he had come back with the cheque. And thanks to friendship, their mismatched personalities, their silent contentions, mattered little and the deal was done. Why the glum-faced dejection?

I have been over the years much caught up with the idea of the Chinese art of commerce. There have been requests to write commentaries in the papers, and invitations to attend conferences and give lectures in business schools. I have enjoyed the journalistic tasks and the academic gigs, but they were a bit of a devil's deal. For in the press and the business school circles the dominant thinking is about the usefulness of guanxi, exactly the view of the Chinese capitalists themselves. The critic is trapped. He has spent so much time arguing why guanxi is no magic, why it works and why it doesn't, that he has forgotten the real issue. The very idea that social relationship is useful and brings profit in business is questionable. In the wider scheme of things, guanxi is a distraction. For what we have to reckon with is guanxi's enormous appeal, its cultural fetishism in the thinking of the media and the business schools and not less the Chinese capitalists themselves.

If you think there's nothing wrong with using social relationships for material gains, think about an Amway party. An invitation to a drink after a parent-and-teacher meeting turns out to be an attempt to sell you something, or to recruit you into the pyramid scheme. It is a touch morally unseemly. Or you can raise the question, as I do with my students: What is the advantage of buying a used car from your uncle, all rainbow tie and fast talking? It is not easy to make a tough bargain when the car yard owner who is also your mother's brother, and he has each year brought you a birthday present since you were so high (your righthand gesturing). In both instances, a certain ethics gets in the way, the social relationship cannot be easily turned into economic advantage or financial gain.

The best approach is to read the great thinkers. For Montaigne self-interest corrupts the purity of friendship. He complains: '[What] we commonly call friends, and friendships, are nothing but acquaintance and familiarities, either occasionally contracted, or upon some design by means of which there happens some little intercourse betwixt our souls.'[3] Before Montaigne, Aristotle had warned of the risk when utility and calculations enter among friends. In *Nicomachean Ethics* Aristotle laid out three types of friendship each with its distinct moral character. Friendship of pleasure is a hostage to vanity and human volatility that invites his disproval. And he thought friendship of utility shallow and 'easily dissolved' as it takes place 'at such a time of life [when people] pursue not what is pleasant but what is beneficial'; he had in mind here trade and commerce. Only friendship of virtue escapes his disapproval, a form of friendship devoted to learning and philosophic meditation. The message is clear: to make use of friendship, or any social relationship, for gain is vulgar and morally hazardous.[4]

In a way, you have to blame Hakka kinship. In Malaysia—and not only among the ethnic Chinese—children are asked to call their elders uncles and aunts. When you have reached a certain age, the salespeople at the shops began to greet you with 'Uncle, how can I help you?', or 'Auntie, we have the latest model, come in and have a look'. You may resent the grovelling and the ageism; but it is meant to be a gesture of respect and there is no insinuation that the salesperson and you are kin related. The Hakka notion of kinship takes this to a greater height. It works by a kind of guile and confusion. To call someone unrelated uncle or aunt, brother or sister is to signal the closeness of your relationship that you are more than friends. In the business world, it says we are so intimate, so entrenched in some common enterprise, and we might as well call ourselves kin. The move is strategic. For what is at the beginning fictive kin becomes overtime real relations.

Hakka kinship is pragmatic and complex. It is a system of enormous freedom. The point is not that those close to us can be treated *as if* they were kin, but their active conversion into real relatives. The principle is: any Hakka person can claim kinship with another Hakka who is not related by blood or by marriage. The result is an instant cementing of previously non-existent social and genealogical bonds.[5]

I grew up watching this anthropological ploy at work. The making of kin was common, yet serious. The guests we entertained, the people we visited in the villages, the adults in the business dinners I was allowed to tag along; they were all uncles and aunts, as I was told to call them. Sometimes I would ask my father a child's question: Why do we have so many relatives? And: Why is that lady my aunt when she is not your sister? The reply would come back: the lady's mother was your grandmother sworn sister; they were very close. The lady and I grew up together, and it right for you to call you to call her auntie. At other times, it was: that man's ancestors came from the same village as ours did. Our families went back a long way. So it was a bit of adoption here, the same ancestral village there, and aunts and uncles were made. No one made too much of it. It is our culture, it is the Hakka custom.

In anthropology, consanguinity (descent from the same ancestor) and affinal ties (relatedness through marriage) define one's membership in a kin group. These are pretty restrictive criteria in determining if a person is our kin. One suspects that, as with much of social life, there is flexibility in actual practice. The Hakka thinking is almost a defiance against the dry formalism. They had gone for the idea that place, adaptation and intimate intercourse are the basis of kinship. The idea of true or fictive kinship seems like fussing over nothing.

As it happens, there has long been a debate on the issue in anthropology. As with the Hakka practice, the question is: Is kinship something you are born into or acquired through marriage, or is it something shaped by the cruder mould of day-to-day relationship between people? John Beattie of Oxford University observed that in many societies people use kinship to describe their relatedness with all manner of people. As though lending credibility to the Hakka custom, many societies in Africa and in Papua New Guinea recognize social ties—based on place, age and occupation—form the basis of kinship. People see kinship in almost entirely in social terms.

> To begin with, a kinship system is not just a collection of distinct and mutually exclusive terms, each denoting a different kind of genealogical and social relationship. It is rather a whole way of life… Often the denotation of kinship terms is not fixed, but depends on the social contexts in which they are used, so that now one, now another genealogical relationship is invoked by the use of the same term.[6]

Kinship is often a metaphor for social bond; it is a way of describing the closeness of a group of people. 'Kinship is the idiom in which certain kinds of political, jural, economic, etc., relations are talked and thought about in certain societies. It is not a further category of social relationships.'[7]

Hakka kinship practices are a form of rediscovery, a way of putting social relatedness to a firmer ground of intimacy. When I say you are my uncle or my aunt—though we are not kin—I am making known the intention that I would like to include you in my innermost circles. The use of kinship terms is like a translation: a 'transfer of significance' from one realm of social meaning to another.[8] It is translation, this declaration of intention, that truly matters in understanding the Hakka custom—not the mix-up about the genealogical or the social basis of kinship.

Free from genealogical bias, the Hakka way of kinship has a distinctive advantage. The whole social field becomes a quarry from which more kinfolk can be mined and admitted to the community. Sometimes the new recruits do not even need to be Hakka speakers. The advantage of Hakka kinship is the advantage of numbers. As social relationships are often useful, people of kinship are even more so because 'they are of family'. The Hakka practice expands the catchment of people who would be valuable to us, who can get us the job we want, who can share with us new opportunities, who would lend us a loan when we need one. It is not all fabrication and communal ruse.

No wonder the values of Chinese petite capitalists are grossly functionalist. And the nature of Hakka kinship helps to explain my parents' ambivalence over something that is in equal measures oppressive and necessary. For my mother, the guanxi-building dinners and meetings ruined her husband's health, but she knew they were important for business. For my father, guanxi is half bunk, half common sense; it does not pass for ethical behaviour. All the same, it is the Chinese or Hakka business way.

Actually, my parents were not easily given over to such mystification. I don't remember the times something like this had happened. Someone—he had just graduated from a university in one of Malaysia's neighbours—had come to meet my father to sell his idea. He wanted to set up a youth wing of the Dabu Hakka association. I was at home during the university vacation, and my interest was piqued. He was young, and his parents had found the money for his education, never mind the fact it was at a Third World university. It would make a good sociological study. But even my father saw through the scam. Forget it, don't go and meet him. The boy is only building guanxi, my father said, as if he was not doing much of that himself.

Yet, a shopkeeper like my father was deep in a mode of commerce that was dependent on social relationships at every turn. Polanyi's idea of social immersion is significant and relevant here. With Chinese petite capitalists, to examine their economic practices is to examine the social makeup of their world. Certainly my father's business dealings were shored up by a web of social connections, though that is not guanxi's only 'use'.

My father's dealing with Iron Monger Lee was to raise capital. The transaction had a quality that was out of the past. It was the old way of doing things, my father believed; it recalled a time when economic life was tied to the obligations of kinship. The graciousness between the two men may have been forced. But it suppressed and moderated their self-interests, and their relationship was left more or less undamaged.

The use of tradition and the exploitation of social relationship in the way of raising capital: it call up a similar story, albeit one grander and more tragic—the story of primitive accumulation.

For Marx the question was asked about the emergence of industrial capitalism in eighteenth century Europe, particularly Britain: how was capital accumulated when there was yet mass capitalist production? The industrial revolution required enormous funds for investment. Primitive accumulation refers to the saving of surpluses from the pre-modern economic forms from chattel slavery to the feudal economy itself.[9] Most notoriously, in England and Wales, the British government brought about a series of legislation starting with the 1773 Enclosure Act that transferred common land to private ownership. The land communally shared and used was transformed into a marketable asset to be bought and sold, and into rent-paying tenancy. One of the effects was to create a new class of landowners who could hedge their land as capital to invest in railways and manufacturing based on the steam engine. This making of capital had drastic social impacts. In a manner both violent and destructive, rural communities were alienated from their traditional livelihood. Their access to common land was denied. And vast areas were depopulated as peasants were forced out and became wage labourers in the factories and workshops: the theme of E P Thompson's majestic *The Making of the English Working Class.*[10] Along with social and communal destruction is another theme. The making of the English working class took place in an environment of resistance and nascent socialist movements of all sorts. Thompson shows the dynamic culture and astonishing political consciousness that propelled them. This cultural and political consciousness had come from its own time, and from the experiences of the social actors. Social and cultural destruction was not complete.

Even without the Marxist polemics, the story of primitive capitalism is worth telling. Capitalism of any form needs to raise capital, and the process is invariably a social process as well. Economic production requires a particular set of social arrangements. For capitalism the production of these social arrangements is as important as the production of goods and services.

The need for funds, and the shunning by the banks had pushed someone like my father towards the 'informal sector' with its own rules of lending and borrowing. This 'informal sector', as I shall describe in other pages, was made up of a plethora of money lenders, pawn shops and people like Iron Monger Lee—people who hoarded money and were ready to play banker. This is not quite the pre-capitalist economy of primitive accumulation. Nonetheless here too was a traditional sector that was a source of funds for those who needed it. And capital raising from this sector involved near byzantine relationships and dealings. Much like as described Marxist notion of primitive accumulation, old relationships were razed and new ones established. Maintaining customary social connections was a clumsy, and at times, painful process; it happened nonetheless. They were all there in what we have witnessed: my father's coy solicitude, the haughtiness of the lender; from the borrower the cringing modesty, the obsequiousness, the sense of belittlement. Like a reluctant pair across the dance floor, the two men had shuffled and steered each other towards the final execution of a financial deal both had desired. The transaction was saved from the social disaster it could easily become.

I have been harsh with the many sins of the small Chinese family business like ours. But half of the time I was struck with the rich social and cultural dealings that filled my father's busy life. His refrain about the 'the Chinese way of doing things' is almost elegiac, which expressed the desire for a world to stay the same while changes were slow and inevitable. But the Chinese petite capitalism also exhibited a good deal of cultural resilience. And a part of this resilience was due to the freedom, the flexibility which the likes of my father brought into their transactions.

In our ethnography, the reading and misreading of the rules of exchange, the wavering uncertainties of Hakka kinship, the etiquette of obligations and reciprocity all exhibit considerable freedom in this regard. Using friendship and kinship for profit has a touch of genius. It has a cultural basis, and its meaning and practical effects are often a matter of context, a matter of communication. It abides to its internal dynamics as much as to the outside circumstances. The problem is the sly functionalism. For one cannot easily turn kinship into profit with moral impunity. Perhaps the truth about Hakka kinship is not the exaggerated idea of usefulness dear to the Chinese petite capitalists. What I had observed was the busy making and remarking of social relationships, some useful, others often not. People took a lot of satisfaction in expanding the network of friends and acquaintances; and the claiming of kinfolk was the highest expression of this undertaking. Functionalism makes us forget that culture and social relationships are important not only because they are useful; they are also valued for what they are—for their intrinsic enjoyment and meaning they give to life, to its sense of import and fulfilment. Chinese petite capitalism, like any form of capitalism, is not only a world of economic relations and materialist considerations. For it to be alive, to sustain the people who populate it, to make possible the mode of economic transactions that defines it—the making of culture is as important as the making of profit.

Imagine, if you will, the scene. A woman stepped into the High Street shop. It was late afternoon, not quite five o'clock. She was hot and sweaty. Perspiration outlined a sturdy body underneath her blue cotton blouse: Auntie Chen was no delicate flower. It was downtime at the shop, dinner still a while to come yet. We were nearing the end of a working day, the pressure had eased off; but with the boss around everyone was fidgety with nothing to do. The woman's entry broke the impasse. Everyone welcomed the intrusion. The shopboys were perked up and my parents' faces broke into a smile. Auntie Chen was an old friend of the family; and since she herself worked in a shop, one selling textile and bedsheets, her breezy way with the shopboys had something of the working-class solidarity about it. They were happy to see her: Auntie Chen, where have you been? She was in her late thirties, the shopboys were mere teens; so she could well have been their aunt. She waved them away and walked towards the long table where my parents were seated. My mother pulled out a chair, while Auntie Chen stooped to take a breath and nodded gratefully. It was the first thing first. She reached into her blouse and retrieved a bundle of cash. My father took the money and put it in an envelope that went into the drawer. The whole proceeding was easy. She was one of our regular depositors, and we would later enter the amount in her account book.

Sitting down, she took out a handkerchief and fanned at her hot face. The shopboys began to gather around her: Sing us a song! Like you did last time! My father looked at her encouragingly; he too wanted to hear her sing. Slow down, boys, she said. Let me take my breath. She got up from her chair, straightened her clothes and gave in to the beseeching.

Folk singing is a major part of Hakka cultural heritage. I had my parents explaining it to me, and I have heard Auntie Chen sing. In November of last year—2018—I went back to the Dabu homeland and did a few things: to check the Yao lineage record, to visit the tourist must-see, the tulou—Hakka walled village an hour's drive away. I also, by chance, encountered two women by the river, their feet dug into shallow water, doing laundry and exchanging sing-song repartee.

To the beat of a wooden baton on the washing, one sang:

> I am young and lonely,
> My dear love, you are far away.
> You are my spirit, you are my soul,
> Do not be corrupted by the city ways,
> Remember you have a loved one waiting for you, longing for your return.

The other woman picked up the refrain:

> Dear Sister, life of a woman is full of sorrow.
> Separation from our loved-ones is our fate.
> Don't be sad. Heaven will bless you.
> Heaven will bring your loved-one back home.

A song of feminist protest, I immediately tagged it. The Hakka people call it shange, folk song or rustic song. Most shange were women's songs, telling women's stories, telling of their bitter lives, their ill-matched marriages. But there were also shange of happiness, of falling in love, or flirtatious bantering with men. In the civil war, Hakka women sang songs of the communist revolution, and songs about joining the all-women guerrilla battalion, an eighty-four-year-old woman in Dabu told me, illustrating her words with a short recital.

Auntie Chen only sang songs of women in love and full of longing. Astonishingly, she was no self-victimizer. Her songs were tough, expressive, joyful.

Surrounded by her young fans, she sang with a strong voice that seemed to hint at the liaisons she had once entered into.

> My man, you have gone to market,
> The men are asking: Why am I showing off my thighs.
> I say to them: I am not showing my thighs.
> I am rolling up my pants, I am crossing the river.
> I am going to see my loved one in the market town.

The shopboys shifted from their boisterous manner and went quiet, like a child calmed by her mother's soothing words. Auntie Chen was such an accomplished songstress, her voice so full of tenderness, that my father put away his paperwork and listened, and my mother was silent. The song seemed to have something for everyone—a touch of eroticism for the shopboys, a reminiscence of love that moved my parents and the senior countermen. It was a peaceful moment rare at the shop: Auntie Chen singing her songs of yearning, the workers and the boss and his wife united in common enjoyment.

Shange recites the Hakka people's rural existence; it celebrates the theme of struggle and survival as they faced intruders and hostile neighbours. And since Hakka women were tough and did not bind their feet—and Hakka custom allowed widows to remarry, there was a rich repertoire of folk songs for women. The women's songs were assertive, often risqué, which makes a statement of sort: Hakka women were no silk-wearing, supine lovers of luxury under men's thumbs. The themes of neglect and grievances came across as a protest. And all this was rendered in Auntie Chen's sweet voice.

Isn't that what culture does at best—to express individual and communal feelings and desires, to give pleasure by celebrating life when it is good, by lightening the sorrow when it is not? Against this listing of culture's pleasure and expressiveness, it usefulness is like nothing. Both culture and utility 'may be thought of in subjective and objective dimensions', the anthropologist Marshal Sahlins writes.[11] Culture is not 'precipitated from the rational activities of individual pursuing their own best interests.'[12] Sahlins is not here advocating an anti-materialist stance. Culture and practical reason both matter in the conduct of social life; they draw on each other for meaning and effects. They are not two separate spheres of human activity.

The ethnography of Chinese petite capitalism is long-drawn, wordy. It is like keeping a ledger. On one side, there are hard-nosed calculations and decisions, financial costs and the returns. On the other side, there are social rituals and etiquette and good manners that threaten to intrude on the tidiness of economic computation, but are in fact a part of it. Something like kinship strains to break out of the prison house of economism. What went on in the High Street shop was a lot of work and production decisions. At the same time, living and business transactions were sustained by custom and the 'the Hakka way of doing things'. As with all small family businesses, the culture of struggle and survival, of hard work and optimism, was everyday being made and remade. Economic production is cultural production as well. The culture of petite capitalist is all dollars and cents, but it is also a source of everyday enjoyment and existential fulfilment; it is what makes petite capitalism tick.

'Hakkaology' may be in its infancy, but the Hakka people's search for their roots has gone spectacularly global in the form of the annual World Hakka Conference. First held in Hong Kong in 1971, the World Hakka Conference had since gone to San Francisco, Singapore, X'ian and other cities. These were grand happenings, attended by people of Hakka descent from all parts of the world. I once went to the smaller, more manageable Toronto Hakka Conference ('One World, One Heart') held at the Canadian city in 2012. The conference attracted delegates from Cuba and Peru, Madagascar and the West Indies—beside men and women from China, Britain, the United States and Southeast Asia. I spent three days going from speech to speech, exhibition to exhibition and met many people. Many of the delegates did not speak Mandarin or Hakka, so the opening ceremony was conducted in English, so were the speeches. At the conference hall there were travel agents that advertised tours to meet fellow kinfolks in Toronto, there were exhibitions of Hakka art and craft, there was a stall that announced its service: Want to trace your Hakka Ancestry, but don't speak/read Chinese? And there were workshops on how to network among the Hakka people and to make business connections in China.

On the final day, I went to listen to a lecture on the magnificent architecture of the Hakka people. The tulou is a system of multi-storey building with an airwell in the middle, surrounded by a nest of individual dwellings reaching upwards. It is an ingenuous built form; it is energy efficient—the airwell draws up stale air and the odour of habitation—and it saves land by the cylindrical built form. The result is a charming communal living in a complex of dwellings in a single building. The lecturer also told his audience,

> The Hakka people were small in numbers, and they faced rough handling by other Chinese – the Cantonese, the Hokkienese, the Sichuanese – wherever they had gone and settled. Tulou were built so that people could live in safety after work, it's a place to escape during an attack. That's why they look the way they do. It is a fortress. It was designed for defence and self-protection.

After the talk, people left for tea and snack being served in the next room. The lecturer stayed on, looking a bit lost, so I cornered him for conversation. He was a Canadian architect teaching at York University—a white face in the crowd of ethnic Chinese at the conference. I told him it was a bit disconcerting to find Hakka study—Hakkaology—was being bandied around at the conference.

There was a lot of searching for roots in the conference, he said. It is a time of identity politics, as you well know. I don't mind all this, he added. The Hakka people are no different from Latinos, or African-Americans in this regard. Oh, yes, there is a lot of talk about building the Hakka network in Canada and the United States, and across the globe. I like the ambition, the idea of a cross-national Hakka community.

I asked him about tulou and how he got interested in it.

For us foreigners, tulou is our entry into an exotic culture, he replied. I've written about it in architectural magazines; and there's a lot of interest among my students. I find the build form engrossing, the mud-brick walls, the communal living, the defence elements of it. We should put some money into research; a fascinating subject—the people, the architecture.

I was pleased with his keen endorsement of a people slowly becoming something of a global community. And I was thrilled by the idea that our forebears were more than labourers and farmers and effete shopkeepers; they were builders, and they were military tacticians who protected their land and defended their families. It went through my mind: Did they, when attacked by bandits and hostile Cantonese, crouch behind the inner walls, open the gate and burst out in ferocious attack, like in some Kurosawa movie? The Hakka the fighter, the military genius: didn't Hong Xiuquan, the Hakka Christian leader, take his Taiping army and captured Nanjing in 1853 and declared it the Heavenly Capital? Our people have political talent too. Sun Yat-sen the founder of the Chinese republic was a Hakka, and Lee Kuan Yew the long-reigning ex-prime minister of Singapore and Deng Xiaoping were all Hakka.

The Toronto Hakka Conference was a celebration of a resilient community whose ancestors had left the homeland to make a better living for themselves and their families in foreign lands. This is a trope of indefatigability easily fallen into one of martyrdom. The Hakka people went far into the wild of Sarawak, east of the Malaya peninsula, to eke out a living in the jungle, as my father liked to tell it. They were poor and they were everywhere looked down upon. And in a sense, the creative freedom of Hakka kinship sits cheek-by-jowl with tulou fortresses as the counterforce that lent the community the dignity they were denied. Culture is a weapon of redemption—not only a tool of guanxi building. For my parents, as for those tulou residents, survival was a triumph and near defeat counted as victory.

This is a powerful expression of a myth. But it is a myth of meaning and communication—not a myth of falsehood. Myth is 'a type of speech', Barthes says, a way of saying something; it carries meaning and it insinuates the speaker's intention.[13] The trouble is myth tends to articulate an ideology that describes the world as natural and objective. For myth to work it must be believable, and it must correspond to what is real or natural or absolute. Myth may be untrue; it is never arbitrary. Myth 'is a type of speech chosen by history', and with an 'historical foundation', Barthes suggests.[14]

The Hakka people—Kejia in putonghua—moved south from the central plain through a series of migrations from the fourth to the thirteenth century to escape war and famine. They settled in the southern regions of China—Guangdong, Fujian, Jiangxi and Guangxi. Later the coolies trade brought the Hakka labourers to the United States, the Americas, Southeast Asia. The term Hakka, the 'guest people', retains the meaning of foreign status in the places where they have settled. The Hakka are not location based but united by a single dialect and dispersed over much of China. The fishing community on Cheung Chau Island where I did fieldwork was Hakka. The merchants on land belittled them for their tatty fishing boats where they and their families lived, but were not above exploiting them by selling them marine engines and diesel fuel and fishing nets. Land-sea division was added to the class-based ethnic discrimination. In Malaysia the Hakka were employed in petty trades—and in the Chinese herbal business—which gave them their low status. Fortunately for us, our parents never took seriously this trope of victimization. Their wisdom and foresightedness muted the brittle social status of working and living in a derelict colonial shophouse. For them everything—well, almost everything—about the Hakka people was hopeful and positive. Their robust 'all good friends are kin' network building pointed to the spirit of a people not let down by their underdog reputation. They were pragmatic and economically astute, but they were not vulgar materialist in their approach to social relationship.

## Notes

1. Karl Polanyi, *The Great Transformation: The Political and Economic Origins of Our Time*, Boston: Beacon Press, 2001.
2. Ibid., p. 48.

3. Montaigne, Michel De. 'On friendship', *The Complete Essays of Michel De Montaigne*. Donald M. Frame (ed). Stanford: Stanford University Press, 1965, pp. 135.
4. Aristotle, *Nicomachean Ethics*. W.D. Ross (ed). Kitchener, Canada: Batoche Books, 1999, p. 127.
5. This feature of Hakka or Chinese kinship is not given sufficient emphasis in the literature. And John Beattie's social definition of kinship is a powerful argument that the Hakka practice is more common and socially valid that it is normally assumed. See: Leong, S. T. 'The Hakka Chinese of Lingnan: Ethnicity and Social Change in Modern Times', in *Ideal and Reality: Social and Political Change in Modern China, 1860–1949*, David Pong and Edmund S. K. Fung (eds), New York: University Press of America, 1985, pp. 287–327. See also: Moser, Leo J. 'The Controversial Hakka: "Guests" from the North', in Leo J. Moser, *The Chinese Mosaic, The Peoples and Provinces of China*, Boulder, Colo.,: Westview Press, 1985, pp. 235–255.
6. John Beattie, *Other Cultures: Aims, methods and achievements in social anthropology*, London: Routledge, 2005, p. 95.
7. Ibid., p. 97.
8. George Steiner, *After Babel: Aspects of language and translation*, Oxford: OUP, 1975, p. 47.
9. Karl Marx, Section 8, *Capital Volume I*. Toronto: Penguin Books Canada Ltd., 1976.
10. E. P. Thompson, *The Making of the English Working Class*, NY: Vintage Books, 1966. See especially, pp. 98–105.
11. Marshall Sahlins, *Culture and Practical Reason*, Chicago: The University of Chicago Press, 1976, p. vii.
12. Ibid.
13. Roland Barthes, *Mythologies*, translated by Annette Lavers, NY: Noonday Press, 1972, p. 107.
14. Ibid., pp. 1–8.

## Bibliography

Aristotle. 1999. *Nicomachean Ethics*. W.D. Ross (ed). Kitchener, Canada: Batoche Books.

Barthes, Roland. 1972. *Mythologies*, translated by Annette Lavers. NY: Noonday Press.

Beattie, John. 2005. *Other Cultures: Aims, Methods and Achievements in Social Anthropology*. London: Routledge.

Feng, H. C. (1948). *The Chinese Kinship System*. Cambridge: Harvard University Press.

Leong, S. T. (1985). "The Hakka Chinese of Lingnan: Ethnicity and Social Change in Modern Times." In *Ideal and Reality: Social and Political Change in Modern China, 1860–1949*, edited by David Pong and Edmund S. K. Fung, 287–327. New York: University Press of America.

Marx, Karl. 1976. *Capital Volume I.* Toronto: Penguin Books Canada.

Montaigne, Michel De. 1965. 'On friendship', *The Complete Essays of Michel De Montaigne.* Donald M. Frame (ed), Stanford: Stanford University Press.

Moser, Leo J. (1985). "The Controversial Hakka: 'Guests' from the North." In *The Chinese Mosaic: The Peoples and Provinces of China*, by Leo J. Moser, 235–255. Boulder, Colo., and London: Westview Press.

Polanyi, Karl. 2001. *The Great Transformation: The Political and Economic Origins of Our Time.* NY: Beacon Press.

Sahlins, Marshall. 1976. *Culture and Practical Reason,* Chicago: The University of Chicago Press.

Steiner, George. 1975. *After Babel: Aspects of Language and Translation.* NY: Oxford University Press.

Thompson, E. P. 1966. *The Making of the English Working Class.* NY: Vintage Books.

CHAPTER 4

# Women's Fate

My father loved his daughters. It had been a joke in the family that he was besotted with his daughters, less so with his sons. I know he was repulsed by the traditional evils of foot binding, concubinage and widow suicide that tied women to their fate in China well into the twentieth century. To my mind he appeared surprisingly progressive. He believed in Chinese customs and values, but he was no cultural fundamentalist. A traditionalist, he was aware of how women should be treated in the modern era. When we teased him about his favouritism, how he had spoiled our sisters, his reply was: They'd have a tough life when they get married and leave home. Let us indulge them a bit. I remember how my request for a subscription of a Hong Kong crime magazine was turned down, while my elder sister got her movie magazines and new clothes for her school outing to Thailand. And he doted on my youngest sister and lavished on her little presents and weekend outings. With the sons, it was: How did the exam go? Or the reminder: You can go to your friend's house, but behave and come home early. I had my father-and-son talks, but they were mostly about studying that I needed to do well in school. Now I can best make sense of all this by saying that for my father, sons and daughters mirrored two different worlds, one of duties and tough decision-making, the other gentle, accommodating and full of affection. His daily chores were hard



S. Yao, *The Shop on High Street*,
https://doi.org/10.1007/978-981-15-2031-0_4

and stressful. And it was natural that he would align himself with the daughters while the sons reminded him of the worries and responsibilities they would inherit if they ever took over the shop. In this division, daughters were pampered and treated with kid gloves and the sons were to be drawn gradually into the business.

I envied my father's easy-going relationship with my sisters; they were indulged and loved. But I now see more clearly the serpent in the garden.

My father had wanted to shield his daughters from the harsh realities when they turned adults and got married. When asked he would say: In the outside world, they won't have the comfort and safety of their own families. Life can be difficult for them with the in-laws. I look back at my two sisters, one divorced and died childless, the other married to a wealthy building developer and settled in the idyllic life of a suburban housewife. Perhaps my father was only half-right in what he foresaw as his daughters' future. Tragedy only makes sense in a morally ordered universe. I know he wanted to protect all his children, not only his daughters. But his efforts were scuppered by the financial stress and a business world where not everyone was playing by the rules, and not everyone was virtuous and fair. To grow up in the High Street shop was to be hauled into a world far from morally ordered and prescribed.

For my sisters too adulthood meant helping in the shop, and sharing our parents' burden and worries. But even they knew they would eventually get married and leave home, and less was expected of them. All the same, they were of the family; if they shared less work than the sons, they could not escape the muddled existence of a Chinese family business. They, like the sons, were hard put to negotiate what they wanted against the demand of the family. For all the siblings, the transition to adulthood felt like a fall from grace.

Theirs was a love match. They had met at a beach picnic to celebrate a friend's birthday. The hostess was three years into a happy marriage, and blessed with an infant daughter, and she had used the occasion to bring her friends together in a half attempt at matchmaking. It was her gift to those less fortunate than she. My elder sister Eileen, who had just started working in an American insurance company after graduating from high school, was not exactly desperate. She was a good looker, everyone said, and quite a catch for any man. She had her men friends, and our relatives had recruited this or that young man for her approval. Meetings were arranged which my parents and Eileen dutifully attended, but they came to nothing. The young men were smart and educated, all from good families. But they were, like Eileen, going through the motions to please their parents. The days of arranged marriages were over, and only the older people had not recognized it.

Eileen had accepted the invitation and gone to the picnic. She was fun-loving, and who could turn down a day on the beach with other young people, feasting on roast chicken and sardine-and-cumber sandwiches, as Mrs Lim had promised? Eileen came back hot and flustered, I remember. She had a good time, and she had made a few friends, she said. We didn't make much of it; we didn't know it was a day that would forever change her life.

When Eileen told us she was bringing a friend home to meet us, we were more curious than excited. We knew she had been seeing a young man for a while, but my parents had wisely kept out of it. When the subject was mentioned, my mother would mutter something like: she is a smart girl, and she can decide things for herself. And my father would run his hand over his short-cropped hair and said nothing. The man who was to eventually become their son-in-law was Wong Peng, a twenty-five-year-old senior clerk in a manufacturer of toiletries. The first time he was brought home to meet us, we found him sweet-mannered and just a little too earnest. We weren't sure if he was suitable for our sister. Eileen could be haughty and liked to do things her way, while he was meek and obliging. Still we didn't hold that against him. Outside her earshot, we brothers joked about how Eileen would keep him on a leash and make him a good husband. And we could not deny that there was a lot going for him. He was ambitious—he had attended night school and got his accountancy diploma, and he was about to be promoted to the post of financial officer. In the end we overcame our reservation and got to like him. When he came to visit us, we children made him an easy prey to our greed, and always managed to extract a few ringgit from him. For my parents, he was uncomplicatedly a person of good character and one earning a good wage.

When their courtship was starting to get serious, one day my father sought him out to say: I hope this is not just a fling for you. I hope you are serious (with Eileen) for I cannot have you hurt my daughter. It must have been a mortifying moment for the young man. No, no, I am serious, I am not frivolous, I have nothing but good intentions towards your daughter, I imagined him saying. Or more likely, he was so stunned as to be left speechless. A lot went on in my father's not-too-subtle enquiry. It was a loving father's intervention, but it was also a pathetic attempt at seeking assurance from one who was all too eager to give it. But then my father was being true to himself. Cautious and practical, he could not put all his trust in love and sentiment. 'Serious intention' was the catchall phrase that embraces a handful of meanings: the young man's pledge of marriage, that he had the means to support Eileen with a degree of material comfort and that during the courtship he would not take advantage of her affection. It was quite a lot to put upon the nervous young man. But then, my father was only taking a page from his own marriage: affection, financial security and the daily tussle of domesticity all matter in a marriage.

The wedding dinner was a modest twenty tables in a restaurant. Our parents and Wong Peng's bicycle-repairer father had opted for a short list of guests of close relatives; neither side wanted a showy wedding. Eileen had wanted a honeymoon in Thailand without the marriage ceremony, but we talked her out of it. The relatives would want to attend your wedding, my parents said to her, and your favourite uncles and aunts who wanted to see you married would never forgive us. The much slimmed-down wedding dinner turned out to be intimate and enjoyable. Everyone had a good time, which foreboded well the future happiness of the young couple.

A few scribbled pages of a worn diary bring back the memories. Patches about the couple's progress—their happiness and contentment, Wong Peng's promotion, Eileen's visits home, our parents' relief. When Eileen told us she was pregnant, everyone was heartened by the good news. We sent over to their house ginseng and other tonic medicine Wong Peng's parents could not afford. A couple of months later she miscarried, and things went downhill after that. A line here, and a line there, the diary's entries recorded the couple's grim-faced visits, my sister's late-night phone call asking to come back, my mother's silence. Then one Sunday morning at the breakfast table the family gathered to talk about Eileen's coming divorce. My mother was red-eyed and teary, my father hid his feelings behind a jumble of words that made little sense. The decision was to bring Eileen home as we weaved our words delicately around the implications.

Against the safe unruffled existence the family had built for itself, Eileen's divorce felt like a catastrophe. Divorce was something happened to other people, those we knew and whose reckless, feather-brained behaviour filled the gossip grapevine. Eileen had complained that the husband had wanted her to stop working, stay home and be a full-time housewife. But those things were expected of any wife, my mother had suggested. In any case, divorce spelt misery for the couple and damaged the parents' social standing. This was happening to us. And the pride we felt for our level-headed existence was shaken.

Over the following days, we prepared Eileen's old room for her return as we tried to come to terms with her divorce. My parents were upset. And my mother's teary eyes said it all. She believed harmony to be the foundation of marriage. Once a woman is married out, her loyalty and sense of permanency should be invested in her marital home. My mother was a stickler for the conventional idea of marriage. But she was resigned to what was happening.

When I asked my father about the divorce, he was full of homespun platitudes. He started to say: You remember the proverb 'Women in marriage is as fallen leaves returning to the soil'? Yes, I remember it, I said. It was a saying that had sent us to uncontrolled hilarity when we first read it in our Chinese literature class at school. I daydreamed furiously that my father would open up. If there was one time to curse heaven and to damn its injustice, this was it. Instead it was the pathetic composting metaphor to describe a woman's fate. Disappointed, he had no poisonous spite against Wong Peng, the in-laws or whoever he thought responsible for bringing about the catastrophe on his daughter. I felt helpless. I was not troubled by the issues that troubled the adults but held little meaning to me—marriage and pregnancy, the shame of marital breakdown, power of gossip. Nonetheless, I felt it was wrong not to confront the couple and get to the bottom of things.

Decades on, I recognize what I had observed in my parents. The timidity, the 'letting things be' resignation, the defence of marriage as the foundation of a productive life—they are the apotheosis of petite bourgeoise values.

My father's saying was a platitude. The set of rhyming couplets clinched its meaning by a rapturous, gardening metaphor.

> Luoye guigen, women in marriage is as fallen leaves returning to the soil;
> Chingjia liye, men's destiny is to be married and build a career.

The philosophic gloss is starkly one-sided. Marriage is women's fate; it is as natural for leaves to return to the soil as it is for women to belong to her marital home. Fallen leaves, luoye, make one think of composting, natural and beneficial for the soil. And guigen, returning to the soil, is full of existential aura. As a metaphor for marriage, it prescribes a woman's sense of arrival. It bestows on her the primordial root of home-making.

Addressing men, chingjia liye, extols too the virtue of marriage but with a materialist twist. If women's destiny is home-making, for men marriage gathers their splintered needs and desires into a single place of responsibilities and male privilege. Taking a wife is a serious business for any man. For the husband home-making is career-making. As marriage is aligned to a man's ambition, a well-matched marriage helps to build his successful career. Who can forget the folksy tale of the virtuous wife, a basket of needle work on her lap, keeping her scholar husband company as he burns midnight oil in preparation for the mandarin examination? There are those who want their wives to stay at home, their idleness a sign of the men's wealth and social status. But the Chinese petite capitalists are of a different breed. For them a good wife is a working wife, one who shares her husband's labour and economic vision.

So much for marriage and men's need and desire. If this has been the final justification of marriage, perhaps Chinese petite capitalism—the institution and the values that sustain it—would explain my sister's failed marriage?

Eileen and her husband lived in modern Malaysia and they worked in the corporate sector. It seems shoddy to blame their divorce on ancient Chinese values. Yet like old habits, traditional codes of behaviour die hard. They have a way of hanging on, of finding new life in the modern conditions. My assessment had been: the meek, pleasant young man had turned rogue once he had settled in the conforming domesticity of marriage. It is as though he had kept secret the unreasonable side of him during courtship. Once unleashed, his desire for Eileen to stop working, to stick to the role of a home-bound wife was a piece with the familiar male privilege of traditional China.

This—the hold of tradition on the living—is true, as far as it goes. Much else had happened in Eileen's journey from marriage to divorce to mental breakdown. We children had variously experienced the everyday stress at the shop, the sharing of our parents' worries and optimism, the uplift and despondency over the takings of the cash register. The women in the family had their own burdens and cosy contentment, however. My little sister was too young, too lavishly loved to be touched by what affected her older siblings. She had been well-prepared for the marriage of wealth and status my father had in mind for his daughters. Both Eileen and my mother, too, had been primed for an easy life. But my mother helped in the shop when she could, watching over the workers at the shop floor. Eileen worked in the kitchen, she and mother discussed what to cook and she set the table and tidied up. She was more or less excluded from the busy proceedings at the shop front. Each time I saw her leaving the shop in the weekend, her face slightly rouged, her sprightly steps signalling a good day ahead at the cinema or shopping mall with friends, I envied her freedom and how the strain of the shop life had not touched her. Always the fizzle of father's words in my head: We have to give her an easier life, for living in her marital home with the in-laws would be different. My father had presumed too much. For to protect the women meant isolating them from the harsh reality of the shop; it required a cloistered existence. My mother and Eileen were, in fact, like the rest of the family, deeply implicated in every aspect of the family business.

The love we have for our parents is never straightforward, my therapist once told me. It nurtures just as often as it oppresses and damages. Children are not innocent. They live with grownups and are alerted to their follies. For them, moral education is often a lot of haranguing from the parents, and as I remember it, a series of warnings about the dire consequences of laziness, of failing the exams, of disrespectful to the elders. But mostly, I learned about my parents' values through hints and hushed mutterings and through a lot of dreadful silences. In our family, we did not confront our parents, and we rarely examined our feelings towards them. They had brought us up with the reticence and quiet wisdom in which they excelled. And the effects were shocking when revealed to us.

Edmund Gosse's late-Victorian classic *Father and Son* was written in an era vastly different from ours.[1] Yet it has a lot of resonance with what Miss Li of the university student health services called the Asian way of childrearing. *Father and Son* is a pained depiction of the contrasting needs and desires of the author and his father, naturalist and preacher Philip Henry Gosse. These contrasting needs and desires drove a wedge in their relationship, as did the social forces that separated the two generations. Edmund Gosse declares:

> This book is the record of a struggle between two temperaments, two consciences and almost two epochs. It ended, as was inevitable, in disruption. Of the two human beings here described, one was born to fly backward, the other could not help being carried forward. There came a time when neither

> spoke the same language as the other, or encompassed the same hopes, or fortified by the same desires. But, at least, it is some consolation to the survivor that neither, to the very last hour, ceased to respect the other or to regard him with a sad indulgence.
>
> The affection of these two persons was assailed by forces in comparison with which the changes that health or fortune or places introduce are as nothing. It is a mournful satisfaction, but yet a satisfaction, that they were both of them able to obey the law which says that ties of close family relationship must be honoured and sustained. Had it not been so, this story would never have been told.[2]

The parents had made Puritan devotion the centre of their domestic life. But the world and its values were rapidly changing. Victorian Christian piety was slowly giving way to dispassionate rationalism and a scientific view of human progress of the Edwardian era.

Edmund Gosse's alienation from his father and his world was gradual. A part of this alienation was due to his deep attachment to his mother.

Emily Bowes was born in London in 1806. She married Philip Henry Gosse when she was in her forties. She was a writer of devotional verses and published tracts on education and moral improvement. A Greek and Hebrew scholar, she made a congenial companion to her naturalist husband. Edmund was their only son. She died in London in 1857, after a protracted battle with breast cancer.

During the late stage of her illness, she took a room close to the doctor's house in London, taking the son with her. Here mother and son received the doctor's visits and waited out the time she had remaining, while the father stayed at home. The young boy was left alone with his gravely ill mother. Edmund Gosse describes the experience:

> I was now my Mother's sole and ceaseless companion; the silent witness of her suffering, of her patience, of her vain and delusive attempts to obtain alleviation of her anguish. For nearly three months I breathed the atmosphere of pain, saw no other light, heard no sound. Thought no other thoughts, than those which accompany physical suffering and weariness. To my memory these weeks seem years; I have no measure of their monotony. … My Father came to see us when he could, but otherwise, save when we made our morning expedition to the doctor, or when a slatternly girl waited upon on us with our distasteful meals, we were alone, – without any other occupation than to look forward to that occasional abatement of suffering which was what we hoped for most.[3]

It is a wretched passage. The suffering, the bad meals, the sullen maid—they are all there. The young Edmund is full of sympathy for his mother slowly dying. Towards the end of the passage, the tone has shifted. The son is lonely and miserable. The bedside watch of his mother is too much for him. He, too, is dying a little. There is nothing to look forward to except—dares he say it to himself?—his mother's final exit from the world.

Decency says we should love our parents, and the closest to love is the sharing of their happiness as well as their suffering. It is simply the nature of the child-parent intimacy. And the young Edmund Gosse must have understood this as he kept watch over his ailing mother: the sense of self-sacrifice as he made her pain his own. The risk of love is the risk of over-identification.

I know this is not of the same league as *Father and Son*, but my mother was often depressed. Being the middle of five siblings, I was close to her. I loved her as any young son would love his mother. Still, as I was growing up, I found it hard to connect my love for her with her unhappiness and the way it intruded on me. I felt almost resentful of her, of this intrusion. Like the young Edmund Gosse, I was befuddled by the double act. To be devoted to one's parents can be oppressive; it calls for a distance—a detachment—from their overwhelming affection.

If this had been for me emotional perplexing and near impossible to resolve, it was all the more so for the women in the family.

My sister Eileen eventually moved back in with the family, and for several years she kept her job in the city. She left early for work, and helped mother in the kitchen when she came home, and retired after dinner to her bedroom. In the weekends she went shopping or to the cinema with her friends—simple urban pleasures of a young workingwoman. However, for all this, she was a different person. We watched her spirit slowly going out of her. Her mood swings intensified. At times, at the dinner table she sat with her dark pinched face, not much interested in the food or the company. Later, after our father died and the shop had closed, she for a couple of years shared a rented house with some friends. But she was often ill and she couldn't keep up with the pace of work at the office. We got her to leave the job and move in with my pharmacist brother Paul in his house at the wealthy suburb of Subang Jaya. We thought it a good solution: she would rest and recover, and she would not be alone. My brother's wife ran a boutique of children's clothes, and she would ask Eileen to do a few chores to make her a part of the family. Grateful for the invitation, she would come out from her room and helped with the packing and sewing on the loose buttons and with re-stitching the lace work.

I stayed with Paul and his family each time I came back from Sydney. I was filled with worries as I entered the house and gave the carry-all to the maid. I asked Paul as he came to greet me: How is Eileen? She is not well, he said. She takes her meals in her room; she hasn't come down for a couple of days. I went upstairs and poked my face into her room. Resting in bed, her hands cupping a steaming bowl of herbal tea, she gave me a feeble smile: Oh, you have come back? Have you had something to eat? With my elder brother in Australia and our parents gone, she was now the most senior in the family, and she was welcoming me home.

When she was diagnosed with breast cancer, she resisted Paul's attempt to send her to the hospital for a thorough medical check-up. He called to let me know his frustration. I phoned Eileen to try to convince her to keep the medical appointment Paul had made for her. But in my mind I was wavering. I felt this was her last grab for dignity, her defiance against a world that had somehow failed her. One day she collapsed in her room and Paul called for the ambulance and admitted her to the hospital. I flew back and prepared myself for the worst. She died peacefully in her sleep; there had been no bedside farewell and all-night vigil over her final hours. It is as though she had made a stand and had kept her ending an affair of her own.

Death in the family is sad yet common. When our father died, an event that brought about the closure of the shop, I felt the foundation of our lives had radically shifted. It happened while Paul and I were still in Adelaide finishing our studies. Upset and harrowed by our father's death, we carried on the best we could. With father gone, my sense of alienation from the High Street shop was complete. At the university I had my discoveries, and found an outlet for my doubts and misgivings in books and in the rowdy gatherings of the student's life—the visit to Miss Li of the student health services was a temporary lapse. I had learned independence, and I was sure the Chinese medicine business was not for me. Western education had made us unfaithful, and the issue of family legacy was easily dismissed.

In contrast, much was stacked against Eileen and my mother. Our father's notion of family love—safe, home-bound and dewy-eyed—was for them, less for the sons. Our father's passing changed everything. The lid on the caldron was lifted. At her more bitter moments my mother would vent her frustrations at how she felt abandoned by his death. It was an expression of grief as much her assessment of their life together. And Eileen fell into a depression the rest of her life.

For Freud, melancholia is a perverse form of mourning at the loss of a loved one. Its lighter symptoms include 'a profoundly painful dejection, abrogation of interest in the outside world, loss of the capacity to love, inhibition of all activities' and general fall in self-esteem.'[4] We recognize these as the features of depression. Mourning is conscious and natural, as one experiences the loss of a love object real and specific. With depression, however, a person grieves for the loss of someone—or something, and the loss can be real or imaginary. And since a person finds the loss intolerable, the internal drama is pushed into the unconscious. Depression is pathological; it is excessive and we might say, melodramatic. Thinking of my sister, I ask myself: How did her mind travel from mourning to depression? And: What had she lost—exactly? What had been deposited in her mind that was so precious when it collapsed it made her withdraw into herself?

The comfort and security of the shophouse, such as they were, ruled our lives. What wondrous intent was built into the humble architectural form. Shop and home, the place of business and the place of domesticity, were one. The intimate blending lent the Chinese shophouse a near mythical power. The shophouse was the centre of fulfilment, everything good and meaningful and financially sustaining resided here; while outside were economic uncertainty and moral fallouts. When the family shop failed, the strings that had tied us to the normalcy of life were severed. But my brothers and I, and my mother and her daughters, felt quite differently; a line was drawn between our approaches to our father's death. My brothers and I were 'socialized' in the shop's daily routines. We helped in the shop after school, with a greater load during the holidays, and we experienced the pressures that faced our parents. Eileen was free from the men's work, but she too could not escape the daily pressures of the shophouse life.

Is it to right to say that, with her childhood happiness and the parental indulgence she had enjoyed, she was not 'toughened up' as her brothers were? Is that why she seemed less prepared for life's rough and tumble than her brothers? The home-bound life had a cost, the cost of a 'streetwise' gutsiness that helped the sons to ride over the tough spots in life when they occurred. Well loved by her father, she had little inkling of the emptiness, of the vulnerability of what he had lavishly invested in the High Street shop. Without the wisdom of doubt, she was unprepared for disaster when disaster struck. At the end my younger sister was rescued by her love-matched marriage, and by her youth—she was fourteen when father died. But her elder sister Eileen was hurled towards the direction of a miserable end.

Ironically it was my traditional-minded mother who, out of her own pragmatism and courage, had more resolutely defied what circumstances had placed upon her.

It is easy to fall into the cliché. My mother had strong hands and sturdy legs, which made me quicken my steps as I walked by her side on the way to the shops. The legend was that Hakka women were renowned not for their beauty but for their willingness to work and share their husbands' labour. In traditional China, so people say, Hakka women's feet were never bound to give them a delicate, arched shape. It was an aesthetic perversion for men of wealthier communities that did not expect their womenfolk to work in the field. My mother was born well past such archaic times. Old photographs show her graceful face and fine cheekbones, and her dark remarkable dark eyes which glint as if holding secrets. In a wedding picture of my parents, she stands firm, her torso upright, that gives the impression of her nudging the groom off the frame. My father had abided to my grandfather's wish that he should marry a tough diligent wife, but he had nonetheless taken a beauty for his bride.

The idea of the hardworking Hakka woman is not all cliché, however. At the High Street shop, my mother shopped and cooked, supervised and cared for the shopboys entrusted to us by their parents. She was a proficient homemaker who, with a stringent budget, looked after the needs of a husband and five children. In the division of labour, domesticity was her terrain and the day-to-day running of the business was left to our father. She said, I just don't have a head for figures. So it was to each according to his or her talent. All the same, despite what she said, she kept a keen eye on the business. She wanted to have her say in how the business was run, and she was not kept in the dark about her husband's plans and decisions.

After dinner, my parents were left to themselves. They talked about many things but always seemed to end up with the shop. Word reached me in my room: words of worries and elation that followed rise and ebb of the daily takes from the sales counter. It was clear to me she could not, even if she had wanted to, seclude herself from the business. After my father died, for almost six months she managed the shop by herself. It was my final term at the university. I took my exams and flew back, and for almost a year she and I worked together to wind down the business. The task brought us closer and made me fear less her dark moods and bad temper. She appeared to me in a fresh light. She was in charge; she was no longer the wife who left the hard-headed decisions to her husband now no longer living. We sat and talked with Mr Tan the solicitor about the best course to take in preparing the shop for closure. She discussed with me which workers should let go first. She took a strong hand in tightening the budget. She took the calls and pacified the creditors and salesmen who needed to get paid. All this she did with a poor head for figures, I felt like reminding her.

And during the shop's remaining months, things happened that alerted me to the situation my mother had been facing for I don't know how long. The boss had died, and a woman was in charge. It invited freedom of all sorts from the workers; they turned garrulous, and they took liberties.

During one particular busy day, the lorry failed to arrive and the bundles of goods were left stranded on the shop floor undelivered. In frustration the foreman, Uncle Pang, had burst out: You should have made the call and reminded them the lorry must come today, not tomorrow. Then the cutting words: You can never trust a woman with important things! I was shocked; I resisted the temptation to front up to the sixty-year-old man, my father's close friend. At dinner, we picked over the dishes we had no appetite for. We could not escape the gloom of the day. She told me this was not the first time Uncle Pang had spoken so roughly to her. She did not want to write me about such things while I was away. Then she gave in to her despondency. I am only a woman, she said, and I have little respect from the men. Her calm demeanour receded, as she gave the lament:

My heart is poorly. I am full of misery. When your father was alive, we worked together and we were a good team. But now … why has your father abandoned me?

My mother took a lot of emotional downtimes in those days. I got the maid to brew her herbal tea to help her sleep. And I used to sit with her in her room with a book (I finished reading Sir Thomas Browne's *Religio Medici* during the night watch hours). She tossed about in her bed, and once in a while her soft voice pleaded me to go back to my room and rest. But I stayed on because I knew it pleased her, and gave her comfort. Over the months, with the new intimacy between us, she began to open up. She told me stories about the goings-on in the shop, about the senior staff. At the end of each telling, she would add: Your were too young, you don't know these things. But I knew, I knew. For I, too, had a first-hand experience of what she was telling me.

It was a common practice among the shops in the neighbourhood. We called it kan dian, watching shop. The idea was to have someone, usually a member of the family, to stay in the shop and act as the eye for the boss when he was away. The aim was to prevent the workers from slacking on the job or pilfering the till or being rude to the customers. More subtly, kan dian was about surveillance and monitoring what was going on in the shopfront. Kan dian reminded the workers the ever presence of the boss now acting through his proxy. My parents may not have read their Foucault on power and surveillance. They nonetheless went for the notion that discipline is best enforced, not by penalties and rewards, but by the ever-present seeing eye of the management. At the High Street shop, the boss and his wife might play surrogate parents to the workers, but they did not trust the workers.

Imagine, if you will, a hot, humidity-laden morning in the tropics, around ten. The shop has been opened since eight o'clock, and by nine-thirty, it is in full swing. Not only us, the whole neighbourhood is toiling and driving the workers hard. Inside the High Street shop, the ceiling fans swirl noisily, frantically. My father has left early for a meeting at the mah-jong club of which he was a member, and someone in the family would be needed to keep an eye on things. Usually the task would fall on my mother, though I had done my share when I finished school.

She parks herself on a wooden stool and faces the sales counter. She is alert. If an older woman customer has been left waiting, my mother would get up and say: It won't be long now. They'll attend to you soon. When a bottle of Rhinoceros Horn Cooling Tonic is needed at the counter, she would pick one from the shelf and hand it over. When changes are needed for a hundred-ringgit note, she would step into the office and return with the small bills. As she watches over the shop, she is keen to give a hand.

In the first morning hours when the mind is fresh, she is full of zeal. It is thrilling to be in the heat of buying and selling, to oversee the turning of merchandise to profit. And it is gratifying to be useful.

Business is good and the clinking of the cash register is assuring. Everyone is working hard. Business rises and wanes. The staff and the boss' wife take a breather, sip their cold tea and wait for the next round of busyness that would last well into midday. Lunch is then served. After a short early afternoon break, at around one-thirty, business picks up again until later afternoon when things peter out.

It is during the afternoon hours when customers are few and work is slow that kan dian reveals its invidiousness. The pace of work is broken, and leisure makes for mischief. It is as though the slowdown has alerted the workers to the hostility—the furtive resentment—they feel towards the boss and his wife. They feign deference, when they speak their eyes do not meet hers. When a customer comes and my mother has brought the item to the counter, Uncle Pang the foreman would ignore it like a bad smell—until the customer points a finger to remind him. And you see the slight twirl on his upper lip that resembles a sneer. With other workers, it is a lowering of the shoulder here, a hard of hearing there. And when the shop is empty of customers, there is open acrimony.

Sitting at the sales counter, Uncle Pang plays his audience like a showman. He is assured of his own skill at telling tall tales. He looks around him: the boss is not here, and he is going to tell the stories about him no one has the cunningness and inventiveness to tell. He runs his tongue over the lips and spits out the words:

The Old Man thinks he is a man of face. He must be running around rubbing shoulders with the filthy rich. He is a small fish and he doesn't know it. How pathetic …

Or: He always holds out the cheques and doesn't pay the salesmen. They say he is stingy and never buys them a decent lunch when they go out together. …

Or: When the ladies come, he puts on his white shirt and comes over to serve them. He thinks he is handsome and irresistible or something …

The men snigger and the shopboys follow them; they laugh with the teller of spite and appear to enjoy themselves. Uncle Pang and his audience are 'talking cock'—the local version of telling cock and bull stories. Normally servile and fawning to the boss, they become bold in his absence. They turned defiant, and the ranting and the rumour mongering were as thumbing the nose at the boss forever hovering over them. The shopfront is men's domain where even the presence of the boss's wife does not count. And since they are too meek to tell such stories before the boss, his wife is the next best target to inflict the pain and vent their anger. With open viciousness the stores are told 'for her benefit'. The boss is the real object of derision, but his wife has bore the hurt and humiliation.

My mother's face is hot and flustered. She is ashamed when she has no cause to feel ashamed. The shopboys she treats members of the family, the foreman Pang whom her children call uncle—they have instigated the cruel putdowns of her and her husband. And she must have asked herself the question: Is it because I am a woman that they have been so open with their insult and slander?

The sales counter called for men's assertiveness. It has no place for a woman or a child. Customers and hawkers and night market traders all wanted to be served by men. The senior staff knew the herbs and they could prescribe for customers simple remedies for their ailments. My mother was the boss's wife but she was not up on the prices of the merchandise, or the medicinal properties of a particular herb. She fared better when a woman customer had asked to see her—the housewife who came for a soup mixture to counter the heat of the June weather, or a mother looking for something to cool her child's high fever. Across the counter was a woman-to-woman talk and sympathy. This, however, was not enough to redeem her from her alleged ineffectiveness.

Uncle Pang's 'talking cock' was classic bullying. My teenage assessment was: he was too cowardly to confront my father, so he picked on my mother. Being a woman was her curse. Pang and the workers no doubt had their grievances, the low-pay and long working hours. Their rebelliousness was surreptitious and cowardly. And I think now whatever subaltern heroism they had display was defiled by their shameful misogyny. For all their anger and resentment, they still put their boss in high esteem, but they could not respect a woman, not even his wife.

The spite and sneers were hurtful, but my mother had put up with them. She would not show her feelings as though not to give the men satisfaction. Misogyny was not a term she used, but 'women's fate' or the long suffering of women. Nonetheless, she wavered. She appeared to have borne too easily the workers' cruelty. And she must also be thinking: Is this a part of marriage, any marriage? If marriage is about sharing—of love, of domestic enjoyment, of child rearing—she was happy to carry the humiliation meant for her husband. It was a kind of sacrifice to take upon herself the bite of the vicious tell-tales, but it did not mitigate the pain she had felt.

For any woman as it was it for my mother, marriage is, as they say, a journey. In marriage, she crosses the threshold and enters another home, the home of her new loyalty, a place where she is bound by a new set of ties and obligations. An former outsider, she has now been made an intimate who shares the hopes and endeavours of the man she has married. This is, of course, the familiar trope of what anthropologists call the patrilocal marriage: the union of intimacy and material interests in the husband's home.

In Marxist political economy, when production is organized around the family, the relations between family members are production relations. Power and exploitation cast a pall over everyone, particularly women. The debate tends to hover around a version of Engels' argument in *The Origin of the Family, Private Property, and the State*. The *Origin* traces the human evolution that led to what we recognize as features of the modern bourgeois family: monogamy, men's authority and men's control of property. The tone is archaic and polemical. The modern bourgeois family, Engels argues, is packed full of ideological predilections. The values of the bourgeois family hold up men's power and privileges, and the final evolution takes the form of the privatization of the family.[5] Each family in its own right and safe within its walls; the family is a hallowed place of sexual intimacy and emotional and economic security. The modern take on the bourgeois family would spin this further. In liberal democracy, the family warrants safeguarding because family values are classic bourgeoise values of property ownership, the triumph of the individual, the family as a consuming unit. The women's role is to contribute to the making of the bourgeois family in this mould.

Marxist historians would seize on this idea in examining the positions of women in traditional China. The anthropologist Hill Gates writes: In late Imperial China,

> women were expected to work hard and live cheaply. … The subordination of women meant that the wealth they produced above and beyond necessary for her own reproduction was channelled to her fathers and brothers, husbands and sons. Women's low status in the Chinese world was not an accident or feudal peculiarity; it was an integral part of a complex economic pattern.[6]

In China's old silk cottage industry, she argues, labour almost totally relied on women in the family. The wives, unmarried daughters and daughters-in-law—they greased the engine of a crucial industry in the Ming and Qing dynasties. The silk industry was organized in the classic petite capitalist mode: home-based, serviced by women's labour, with men making the major decisions. It was an industry that fortified the Chinese patrilineal family where women were 'a source of power, wealth, and social superiority for Chinese men'.[7] And it was ideological to boot. Since silk production relied on home-bound wives and daughters and daughters-in-law, domestic confinement became a primary feminine virtue. The Confucian propriety that dictated the feminine propriety of women turned out to be one of significant economic logic.

The Marxist analysis is at its weakest when it deals with private sentiments and sensations—love, sex, appetite, pleasure. Family and marriage are nothing if not these things as well. It is not wrong to say that Chinese patriarchy had made women a source of men's wealth and social superiority. This however is only half the truth, and may be not even that. For home and marriage also create mutual dependencies and common interests that propel family life. This is true in contemporary times and, one suspects, it was true in late Imperial China.

Speaking of wives: in most marriages, it is not easy to exploit one's marital partner in the way you can exploit strangers and distant kin. The carnal tenderness and gracious negotiations give the husband-and-wife bond a real emotional depth. (Even in a bad marriage, not everything is unredeemable.) We are, of course, talking about the nature of intimacy. Intimacy is a tryst of give and take, and it sets the 'flows and transitions between bodies [and] selves' and 'forges distances and proximities as well as bonds and attachments', the anthropologist Ann Stoler has put it.[8] The culture of sharing and negotiation dominates a marriage. And in property relations, joint ownership is guaranteed by modern law. (My mother's name appeared in the will as one of two owners of the High Street Chinese medicine business.) In Chinese petite capitalism, its complex social arrangement gives women their due in all kinds of ways, even as it disparages their poor decision-making and other weaknesses. Patriarchy is not undone, but moderated.

At the shophouse, we children were not privy to everything that went on between our parents. To our eyes, they had chiselled out a closeness in the stress and chaos of the family business. They talked, they parleyed and they rankled. The silk industry in Imperial China is one thing, at the High Street shop everything pointed to ambiguous effects of the unholy coupling of patriarchy and petty capitalism. And certainly with my mother, marriage had made her investing in an institution arguably designed to repress and exploit her. My mother was not insensible to the preserve of men—her husband, the foreman and the senior workers—she had to work with. All the same, she was not wrong in holding dear the social and financial security that the marriage had provided her and her children.

Hakka folk legend boasts that a man should choose a wife a woman of strong body and strong legs. By then even petite capitalists fell in love, and some passionately with the women they had married and bore them children. The solidarity of marriage could be a conspiracy of patriarchal swindling. But it could also be a means for someone like my mother to negotiate a stake for herself and her children in a joint economic enterprise.

Patriarchal oppression had borne heavily on Eileen and my mother, placing them inside the cove of the domesticity and over-protection. But they were also extravagantly loved, they were not neglected emotionally. In contrast my brothers and I had gone away, and the experience had been a mixture of homesickness, self-realization and intellectual discovery. Towards the end, after graduation, I could barely make myself leave the new home I had made in Adelaide; only filial responsibility had made me come back. We sons were, as far as I can remember, encouraged to think big, which in petite capitalist terms means helping out in the shop and studying hard at school in order to make something of ourselves. The expectation was oppressive yet enticing. We were pushed to succeed, for ourselves and for the pride of the family. This pressure was not applied to our sisters, not in the same degree or in any sustained fashion anyhow. And how we sons had struggled against the doubts and the fear of failure in meeting what were expected of us. I believe it was quite different with our sisters. As soon as they showed poor performance at school, the pressure was off. If they couldn't get to the university, there was always the secretarial school and the local college. Eileen never found that inner solidity that education and parental pressure had helped to build. It is the best articulation of the gender prejudice that still persists in the world of Chinese petite capitalism.

About my mother, it could be said that she was similarly cocooned and protected. Compared with her daughters, though, she had put up a great deal—the spite and sneer of the workers, the singlemindedness of her overambitious husband, her older children veering towards independence. But she was older and tougher, and she was of a different mettle from her daughters. All the same, she, too, had hung on to the comforting edifice of the shophouse as home and a place of security. Her husband's death was the dead knell of what the shophouse had offered. What had been the centre of her life—the High Street shop, her emotional investment in it, the stability of a marital life, her dependence on a man she had deeply loved—were turned to ashes.

My sister Eileen's unhappiness and my mother's sense of abandonment after her husband's death have been a difficult subject. What happened to them is not in the same league as the ambitions and economic scheming of my petite capitalist father that filled the pages of the book. I remember the wretched passage from *Father and Son*: Edmund Gosse depiction is not merely 'sad', it is full of regret and self-questioning. The thought must have come to him: How awful it is to resent one's mother. Have I done justice to her suffering when words are blunt instruments to lend truth to human suffering? If philosophy is our aid, it just as often casts doubt on our intellectual enterprise. There seems always 'more' that lies outside our writing and conceptualizing.

Like the author of *Father and Son*, I half wanted to escape the suspicion—if I look deep enough—that I had somehow been a part of what had fallen upon Eileen and my mother. I had been relatively immune from what they had suffered. I felt lucky, but also a sense of shame. The last weeks before I left Adelaide, my mother's urgent letters in my jacket, my girlfriend Virginia and I had driven to a hotel in the Adelaide hills and over the sleepless night tried to coax a future out of our precarious but cosy existence. At the end, I thought it best I went back. How tempting it was, urged by love of another kind, to abandon my mother and others still at home! The love and filial loyalty I had for my mother was a pencil line away from being betrayed. If Eileen's and my mother's misery had its origin in the patriarchy of Chinese cultural tradition, my relatively freedom was male privilege, which made me complicit in their undoing.

And parental affection sometimes seemed to guarantee little. Loved to excess, my younger sister was destined to live the charmed life my father had imagined for his daughters; my elder sister, faced with her marital breakdown, was unprepared for the pain and the damages that followed. Chinese petty capitalism is prone to turn daily struggle into virtue. Daily woes may be stressful, but they got the family to buckle up and do their best. There is little room for the talk of defeat in this narrative. Women have a special place in this telling. My mother and my sisters had, each in her own way, borne the costs of living in the High Street shop. But what were the costs, exactly? The financial stress, certainly, and the worries of bills unpaid and dashed hopes. My mother once told me she knew too much about the goings-on shop, and she would rather have known less. She felt vulnerable, she said. She was the boss's wife, but she didn't have the tough authority, the leverage of a man, to handle the workers. As for my sisters, they helped in the shop, but they were also primed for a life as married women. Their future was elsewhere, in their martial homes. My father's good sense nearly betrayed itself. As often with women in Chinese family business, larger issues hovered like ghosts over their lives.

## Notes

1. Edmond Goose, *Father and Son*, London: William Heinemann, 1909.
2. Ibid., p. 1.
3. Ibid., pp. 58–59.
4. Sigmund Freud, 'Mourning and melancholy' in *Collected Papers*, Ernest Jones and James Strachey (eds), NY: Basic Books, 1939, p. 153.
5. Something a social worker or a police officer investigating domestic dispute would recognize.
6. Hill Gates, 'The commodification of Chinese women', *Signs*, 14(4), 1989, p. 802. See also the same author, *China's Motor: A thousand years of petty capitalism,* Ithaca & London: Cornell University Press, 1996.
7. Hill Gates, 'The commodification of Chinese women', p. 832.
8. Ann Stoler (ed), *Haunted by Empire: Geographies of Intimacy in North American History*, Durham: Duke University Press, 2006, p. 472.

## Bibliography

Freud, Sigmund. 1939. "Mourning and melancholy'". In *Collected Papers*, edited by Ernest Jones and John Strachey, NY: Basic Books, pp. 151–62.

Gates, Hill. 1989. 'The commodification of Chinese women', *Signs* 14 (4): 799–832.

Gates, Hill 1996. *China's Motor: A thousand years of petty capitalism,* Ithaca & London: Cornell University Press.

Gosse, Edmund. 1909. *Father and Son*. London: William Heinemann.

Ann Stoler (ed). 2006. *Haunted by Empire: Geographies of Intimacy in North American History*, Durham: Duke University Press.

Sertaç Sehlikoglu, and Aslı Zengin. 2015. Introduction: Why Revisit Intimacy? *The Cambridge Journal of Anthropology* 33 (2), Autumn: 20–25.

CHAPTER 5

# Shop-Floor Heroes

The bodies on the low-swung canvas beds were as drunken revellers at rest; or less happily, as dead hogs laid out in rows by tribesmen after a hunt. It was around midnight, and I had just come back from a late movie. I inserted the key into the chunky lock and opened the door. A dim light had been left on for me, and I saw the shopboys, some deep at sleep, some twisting and turning, mouthing words from the dregs of dreams. It was too hot for blankets, and each body showed itself with a grubby pair of singlets over the torso, while the lower limbs sought decency in a pair of pyjama pants. They had worked hard; they had eaten to the full the simple dinner at the shop. A dormitory had been made from the shop floor, where they slept and rested. I heard the soft rustles of the shopboys on their beds, but they were too tired to detect my presence. I walked by and let them sleep, and found my way up the staircase to the living quarters upstairs.

I knew the boys and their dreams. They were three or four years older than I, friends and mentors to this twelve-year-old who shared with them the ordeals of growing up. I was the boss' son, they were our workers. But at night, when I had done my homework and joined them at the shop-floor-turned dormitory, we were just a bunch of teenagers doing the things we did. I was there most nights. Dinner was over, and the shopboys lay out their canvas beds, each claiming a spot at the shop floor. Some were dressing to go out, most fidgeting over their beds—stretching the sheets, buffing up the pillows, making themselves comfortable. I remember well these



S. Yao, *The Shop on High Street*,
https://doi.org/10.1007/978-981-15-2031-0_5

evening hours. Away from the bosses, the talks were free, the jokes rabid and juvenile. We reviewed the movies we had seen, evaluating each for the ferociousness of salon fistfights for Westerns, and by the blood-drawing kung-fu bouts for Hong Kong martial art epics. We gauged the voluptuousness of the new girl at the coffee shop opposite: Was her chest of the 'pork bun' or 'hamburger' magnitude? We assessed the strength of the bully working at the hardware supplier three shops down. Someone said: We'll kick him up the arse next time we see him, then waiting for others to work out the logistic of the assault. It was a fierce, undisciplined world we had created for ourselves.

I say 'we', actually it was they talked and I listened. When I added: 'Yes, we should do this', it was a way of claiming comradeship with the shopboys. The sleeping quarters was their domain to which I was pleased to be admitted. Those who have lived in a dormitory—ask any ex-boarding school student—remember the joyless monastic existence. Here, though, things seemed different. Here they talked exuberantly without care; here they dreamed of things teenage boys everywhere dream about.

The shopboys came to us from small towns and villages on the outskirts of Kuala Lumpur. Their parents—fellow Hakka kinfolk—had sent them to the High Street shop to learn a trade or to take them away from various mischiefs they were up to back at home. They were poor scholarly materials—failing at school was another reason for them to be sent to our shop. At the shop, they were given a small stipend and provided with makeshift accommodation. Depending on how you looked at it, life at the shop was reasonable, not unpleasant. Board and lodging was free. And working in the shop gave them a taste of the city life. There were the cinemas and shopping malls and karaoke lounges, and fast and easy friendships were made with other shop assistants—other boys and girls—who worked in other places. With these urban pleasures and opportunities, they were happy to leave behind the farm work, the job in a garage, the dish washing at the food stall they did back at the townships and villages.

My father called the shopboys apprentices which lent their work a degree of importance. This was his bid to their parents: the boys would do the chores, but at night they would study to become healers, and perhaps one day open their own shops. However, self-study required discipline and a level of language proficiency the boys did not have. Learning and remembering the names and the medicinal qualities of the herbs was tough going, and the shopboys soon gave up. I could count on the fingers of one hand the number of boys who actually realized the petite capitalist dream. For most the High Street shop turned out to be a temporary sojourn, one they eventually left to pick up the many petty jobs offered by the city.

Still, I do not think the time they spent living with us had been a waste. Each time one of them decided to leave, my father would begrudge their decision. He said: Why don't you stay and learn the business? I've promised your parents that you would be making something of yourself. My father's sour tone said it all. But in my mind, there was no let-down and disillusionment in the future of my shop-floor comrades. They were free, and they could just pack up and leave. They had seen through my father's endorsement of an existence whose rewards and veracity I was beginning to doubt. They had survived the shop; they were thrilled by the city and could take up any job they liked out there in the world. Surely that counted for something?

I sometimes came upon them in the street. Since leaving the shop, they had taken up peddling in night markets, they had been waiting in coffee shops, or working in car repair shops. Sometimes I saw one of them, his soiled singlet having given way to a white shirt and black tie, demonstrating a brand of food processer in the shopping mall. Across the car park on my way to school, for many months I came upon the young Xiao Fu, Little Tiger: the moody kid who took me to see *Master of the Flying Guillotine* at the Madras Cinema, which later sent me to dreaming of decapitating our schoolyard bully in mid-air. Xiao Fu had become the leader in a team of jaga kereta boys, who washed and waxed and looked after your car while you were shopping or at work. He gave me a shy nod when I passed by. I looked back at him: he had an odd, unhinged look, like one lost his way and can't find his way home. I couldn't work it out. Later, someone told me Xiao Fu had got a heroin habit. Perhaps 'chasing the dragon' was his way of thumbing his nose at his parents, and the empty existence at the High Street shop, I am not sure.

For Xiao Fu as for the other shopboys everything began at the shop-floor-turned dormitory. It is as though the dormitory at night was a prison or a detention camp where rebels organized themselves and honed their revolutionary skill. The boys' blustering and bragging—it was their way of coming to terms with their troubled lives. As they settled in their canvass beds, their dreams and yearnings were mixed up with what they saw and experienced at the shop. They had put the High Street shop to a gruff assessment. The shopboys held for me a certain romance. My parents were proud that they treated the boys as members of the family. They were their surrogate parents in the city. But the shopboys had busted the myth. I like to think that their departures were more than an escape, but a rejection of the paternalism so much a part of Chinese petty capitalism.

In Chinese petty capitalism, management benevolence has grown out of a certain idea, a certain ethos. At the High Street shop we were proud that the workers were treated like members of the family. The shopboys were our kin, and they had been put under our care so that they could better themselves. It was an obligation of kinship. Their parents had entrusted them to us, and we would do for them what we could. My father would teach them about the Chinese medicine trade, and my mother would do little chores for them—sewing a loose button on their shirts, brewing them herbal tea when they were sick, coaxing them to sip another bitter mouthful as would their own mothers and giving them little presents to take home during leave. And it made sense that they would eat with us. Breakfast, lunch and dinner were served at a big round table at the back of the shop but within sight of the sales counter, so that someone could down his chopsticks to serve the counter when a customer turned up. The morning and midday meals were simple fare of rice porridge with dishes of pickled cabbage and salted fish and boiled peanuts. Dinner consisted of a chicken and a pork dish, a soup, and plates of vegetables boiled or stir-fried and garnished with coriander and light fish sauce. Evening meals were served early, around six, so that the senior staff—the foreman, the counter salesmen, the part-time accountant—could eat and go back to their families. A sense of egalitarianism prevailed at the table. We shared with the workers the same rustic dishes. If taste could give a message, these were meals of common purpose and befitting of the way we lived and worked. Rice porridge, pickled cabbage and salted fish were the staples of labourers and lorry drivers, quick and frugal meals for people who had little time to waste. From breakfast to dinner there was no lingering at the table after we put down our chopsticks. My father tried to whip up a conversation, but the effort felt false. People were in working mode even at the dining table, and besides who could relax with the boss around?

Still, the shopboys and the senior workers were practical people. The meals came with the job; eating in the shop was convenient and saved money. To speak of power and paternalism seems overstating the point. Yet, the truism 'there is no such thing as a free lunch' makes a bid even at the modest dining table of a Chinese shophouse. The workers and the boss were playing their part; their behaviour followed a certain script. The boss was the leader, a figure of authority, and the workers were the recipients of his benevolence. The meals were free; yet you felt they had to be paid for somehow—by gratitude, by a hat tip to the boss' largess, by an expression of respect.

Chinese petite capitalists pride themselves on enjoying a special relationship with their workers. It is a relationship full of goodwill and folksy charm. At the High Street shop, what little truth there's in it, however, was diminished by how it actually worked. The countermen and the other senior workers had been with for us for a long time, and the young shopboys were sons of the uncle and aunties of the Hakka tribe. They were more than workers; they were family. What was behind my parents' thinking was a mishmash of Confucianism and Buddhism and kinship that defined the plain decency in how they treated their workers.

Paternalism is an old cultural trick. Anyone with a little political sense can easily see through the double act. Charity generates gratitude from the poor and ties them to the giver—always a powerful and wealthy man or woman who needs to dispense the handout for his or her vanity, kindheartedness and sense of doing good for others. As with political power, bread and circuses always prove less costly and more effective in the long run than coercion. Charity is about bribing the poor; it is also about instilling in their everyday habits the idea of the benignity of the powerful, as Gramsci would say.[1] The Chinese petite capitalist version of this is: To get good work out of the workers, fair treatment and kinship are the better guarantee.

On charity and the sense of gratitude it brings the rich, Oscar Wilde writes in *The Soul of Man Under Socialism*:

> We are often told that the poor are grateful for charity. Some of them are, no doubt, but the best among them are never grateful. They are ungrateful, discontented, disobedient, and rebellious. They are quite right to be so. Charity they feel to be a ridiculously inadequate mode of partial restitution, or a sentimental dole, usually accompanied by some impertinent attempt on the part of the sentimentalists to tyrannize over their private lives. Why should they be grateful for the crumbs that fall from the rich man's table?[2]

The charity of the rich is morally tainted. The upper hand of power wears velvet gloves. Indeed, 'Why should [the poor] be grateful for the crumbs that fall from the rich man's table?'[3]

My father thought it was right to be kind to the workers, to treat them fairly. He wanted his workers to prosper, and he was pleased when one of them went on to a better job or started a shop of his own. He was certain that their success was due to him and to the time they spent in the shop. Yet, he would just as likely go back on his own words and betray the kindness he lavished on the workers.

Looking back, it's a bit of a shock to realize my parents did not trust the workers. The management style of Chinese family business relies on silent censures and insinuations; workplace discipline is maintained by ostensible civility. My father never shouted at the workers, or openly reprimanded them for the mistakes they had made. I see all this now with a less innocent eye. Things were not what they seemed. Some practices come back to me which I recognized even then for the hurt and embarrassment they had caused.

When a worker had resigned and prepared to leave, he did the usual things. He packed his things, he said his goodbyes, he got the bonus and a pep talk from the boss. If there was a good story to tell about his departure—he was getting married, he had found a better job, he was moving back to his village to help in his parents' shop—it would go around like the bottoms-up cheers in a dinner party. When the worker simply wanted to leave, it hinted at his hatred for his work and everyone kept silent. And the farewell ritual quickly moved on to the next stage as he was about to step off the premises.

Let's say it was a typical tropical afternoon, hot and steamy. Perhaps a slight breeze had picked up, I don't know, to nudge the proceedings along. The young man had changed from his singlet and dark cotton trousers into a clean polo shirt and a pair of stiff cargo pants, looking like someone going on a holiday. But he looked nervous, and defiance sat on his upper lip where the shade of a beard was growing. He turned to the boss sitting behind the long iron-wood table by the office and shoved the bag towards him. It was a part of the ritual and he knew what to do. He should have unzipped the bag to show its content, but that's not the how it was done. Earlier the boss had given him the pay and bonus in a red envelope, adding his best wishes and a few words of encouragement. And the boy conveyed his parents' gratitude: the boss had turned their son from a youngster to a working man. The young man looked on, and the boss proceeded to do what he had to do. He dipped his hand in the bag, and for a brief moment—it must be seconds, but felt longer—fingered blindly the inside, and withdrew. It was done very quickly, surreptitiously. And I remember that on every occasion nothing suspicious was found, no thefts were discovered. The probing hand entered and left; inside were soiled laundry and some CDs, some books and trinkets. Why go through all this? But there was no need to ask the question; it was just a custom, I should not make too much of it. Yet however delicately executed, the going through the bag was an accusation. It said: The man might be pilfering and had to be stopped. It was a warning for all those present. Each time I witnessed the ritual, it never failed to impress me the cold fury in the departing worker's eyes, the cold fury of a man wrongly accused and misjudged. My father kept his placid face; he could barely look at him in the eyes.

Every worker had to go through the ritual when he made his leave. My father may be unfairly suspicious; actually there would be at any given time a bit of thieving going on in the shop. The cash in the till would sometimes fall short, and a carton of Tiger Balm or Scott's Cod Liver Oil capsules—items easily turned into cash—would go missing. It could be theft, or it could be a sabotage by a disgruntled worker. The bag-checking was the last opportunity to catch a thief, but it was rarely about that. Analytically, it was a display of management power at its most arbitrary and invasive. It was as though the boss' kind deeds and benevolence called for a counterpoint, lest he be taken for granted. Something had to be added, something of real bite, something with a real force of deterrence.

The shophouse is a building, a colonial form of architecture; it was more interestingly a social order. As a social order, it consisted of the shopkeeper and his family, the foreman and the salespersons who served at the counter, and the shopboys who numbered from six to eight at any given time.

The shopkeeper was the petite capitalist proper. He was the head of the family, and everything he did and said signalled his authority and the fact of his ownership. The mid-level staff had learnt their trade elsewhere and were 'head-hunted' by my father—a mutual poaching of staff common in the Chinese medicine business. In outlook and ambition they aligned themselves with the boss; and the most ambitious among them did not conceal their ambition to leave and open shops of their own. The leader of the counter staff was the tou shou, the headman, the dark-faced Uncle Pang in his late forties. He was second-in-charge next to my father. The shopboys called him Two-Faced for his alternating charm and scowling when serving different customers. Pang taught me about bad faith. He was close to my father; they considered themselves friends, but he gossiped about the boss and poked fun at his misdemeanours, real or made up. On the whole, the counter staff worked hard and took order from my father. They were street-wise men, sophisticated and slippery. Nonetheless, a certain prudence was observed by both sides. Management orders were dished out, and workplace recalcitrance did not get out of hand. The shopfront was a place of uneasy peace, where work was done with fair efficiency.

The shopboys were on the lowest rung. For them the shop floor was the lower depth of labour and tedium and poor wages. Young and restless, they found little appeal in the 'from shopboys to shopkeeper' petite capitalist dream. They came from families of the rural poor. Their parents were farmers, tradesmen, stall keepers, car upholsterers, restaurant workers. At night, stories about their juvenile misdeeds went around the canvas beds. Some had been gang members; some were petty thieves and sought escape from the police; growing up problems got mixed with class disadvantages. But their banishment to the city was a blessing. There were opportunities and urban pleasures they could only dreamt about in the small towns and villages. The boss' benevolence may be oppressive, but it lightened the homesickness and the tedium of work at the shop. For most, the shop-floor dormitory opened up the vista to a new life, to a sense of opportunity and discovery.

Dormitory living calls up the image of a British boarding school, with glum-faced children separated from their parents; or a hospital, or a detention centre, each a place of bureaucratic meddling and surveillance. It is a subject that fills the academic literature. The sleeping quarters on the shop floor is not quite the 'total institution' of Irvin Goffman or Michel Foucault's panopticon in his study of the origin of the modern prison.[4] The idea needs a lighter touch. At night, the shopboys would make the shop floor a place of their own. Here they were relieved from the boss's oppressive presence, where they could rave and bluster and be themselves. Yet, the air of confinement never totally vanished.

Remarkably the accommodation at the High Street shop found a kindred arrangement in petite capitalism elsewhere, in early twentieth-century Britain.

The historian Christopher Hosgood, writing on the Edwardian British retail trade, notes: '[The] relationship binding clerk to employer was a strongly paternal one in which, while clerks served loyally, employers were expected to provide protection and security.'[5] This is for us familiar territory. Like our shopboys, the clerks of Edwardian retailers found their work harsh and enfeebling. Their customers were genteel, middle-class women easily flattered by civility and good manners. The British retailers, too, provided live-in accommodation for their junior staff. Hosgood is certain that it was designed to break the separation of 'work, sleep and leisure', and take away workers' sense of independence and self-worth.

> The living-in system perpetuated a social arrangement that broke down the barriers separating the three primary spheres of life: work, sleep, and leisure. All aspects of life were conducted in the same place, or under the same authority, and a shop assistants' daily routine was carried out in the company of like individuals performing similar tasks, under a well-organized system …
>
> The conditions for those living in were by many accounts spartan at best and unhealthy at worst. More important, perhaps, living in imposed a series of petty regulations, further subordinating the assistant to employer and thereby perpetuating the authority exercised during working hours. The end result was that assistants were stripped of their ability to deal effectively with the outside world. A lack of privacy undercut shop assistants' individuality.[6]

Hosgood calls the living quarters upstairs at the shop 'mercantile monastery', a fraught and pregnant phrase. In the Edwardian social order, the retail clerks were not gentlemen. They did not have their own homes, and their gentleman status was a fake, a sad put-on. The women who worked on the same premises fared no better. They lived above the shop as well, but men and women were segregated. The living-in accommodation provided no opportunities for friendship—or any kind of relationship—across the sexes. The result was to compromise the sexual identities of men and women alike. Hosgood concludes: Thwarted of their masculinity or femininity, and kept within their separate quarters, the shop assistants 'entered a stage of suspended adolescence'.[7]

The High Street shop was no Edwardian draper-retailer. Its workers were men and boys. They lived in a contemporary modern city, and they did not suffer sexual segregation and forced celibacy as did the Edwardian salesclerks. The idea that the shop assistants 'had few opportunities to escape their master's influence outside the workplace' doesn't resonate here.[8]

Yet for all that, 'mercantile monastery' remains a potent idea—when we broaden its meaning, when we see it as fostering a system of denials that put under stress the shopboys' lives and aspirations.

At the High Street shop dormitory at night, monastic seclusion was never complete. Shopboys went to the cinema or left to meet friends at the Indian tea stall, and they returned and brought news. The buoyant sprit of their night out was infectious. Those who had stayed wanted to know: Did Jet Li do his 'no-shadow kick' (in the movie)? Has Ah Liew got a job yet? Did you drop by at Sakura (karaoke lounge) and check it out? If the dormitory was monastic with its canvass beds and austere living, it was also a place of freedom. Here they talked freely, exuberantly. It was an hour or so before bedtime; the dim light cut them off from the outside world. With no more need to put on a civil front, they bantered and told stories amongst themselves. The shop floor at night abetted certain thoughts, a certain consciousness even, but it's hard to know what it was exactly.

In any big city you meet people like our shopboys but we barely notice them as we go about our business. They are unremarkable and invisible, like the person behind the ticket booth at a busy train station. What is striking, though, is their sheer number. Strolling through any Southeast Asian city, the shop-floor young men and women are so numerous as to resemble an army of workers who fill the high fashion boutiques, the hair dressing salons, the supermarket check-outs, the promotion kiosks and mobile phone stalls at the shopping mall. There are the 'new proletariat' of the urban economy. They do not own the shop or stall where they work. They are mobile, they change from petty job to petty job, and they dream the dreams that always seem to elude them. Multiply them by the tens of thousands, you begin to see of them as a social group, even a class, united by their common character, by their common need to ram against the circumstances and their crushing effects.

At the High Street shop the nightly ranting and telling of tales were crude exercises in self-scrutiny. The shopboys were trying to work things out: the boss' patronizing style, their future in the city, and the question—should we stay, or leave for better jobs elsewhere? Hosgood's is the work of a social historian. But there are also the writings of H.G. Wells who left a vivid account of his years working as a draper's assistant. This from his memoir *Experiment in Autobiography*:

> I had to straighten all [the] stock and pack it up after it had been shown and put it back into the proper fixtures; I had to measure and refold it when the manufacturers delivered it, to block it or to roll it in rolls. This blocking, rolling and folding was skilled work that needed a watchful effort I gave grudgingly, and I never learned to do it swiftly and neatly. You cannot imag-

> ine how maliciously a folded piece of sateen can get askew, how difficult it is to roll huckaback, how unruly a fat blanket is to pack up and how heavy unwieldy pieces of cretonne can be when you have to carry a score or so of them up narrow folding steps and adjust them neatly on a rising pile. My department also included lace curtains. These had to be unfolded and held up by the junior apprentice while the sales-man discoursed to the customer.[9]

The repetitive tedium of the work aroused strong emotions in the young Wells.

> As the heap of tumbled curtains grew and the customer still wanted to see something a little different, storms of hatred and revolutionary fervour went on behind the apathetic mask of the junior apprentice, doomed before closing time to refold them all and put them away. … [T]hose two years of incarceration [were] the most unhappy hopeless period of my life.[10]

It is a bitter condemnation of the petite capitalist trade. Wells' novels are filled with characters who are trapped in their jobs and their need for escape, clearly a reflection how the young Wells had felt. Mr Polly in the novel that bears the name, and Mr Hoopdriver in *The Wheel of Chance* are feeble men who try to rise above their station by guile or by the force of fantasy.

Incarceration and escape form the dominant trope that describes the shop assistants' lot in Edwardian Britain. It is the same trope that calls up the life of the shopboys at the High Street shop, and it makes me think of the shops and stalls and backyard factories in a sprawling neighbourhood in Phnom Penh, Cambodia, that I chanced upon during my visit. I noted the pots of hot soup over the stove, the sound of hammering and banging from inside the workshop, the assembling of plastic flip-flops inside a hardware store, and my eyes took in the young boys and girls like our shopboys. The dormitory living had gone. But if you were lucky, you could catch them at lunch time sitting at a rackety mah-jong table and sharing the meal with the family who employed them. Mostly, they were lost inside the dark of the dingy premises. It was the same scene I had encountered in the back alleys in Guangzhou, or in Old Delhi—the same rickety shops, the same army of boys and girls, men and women, busily working and invisible to the passers-by. At these places, an idea often came to me: what would happen if these boys and girls, these men and women, downed tools and left their jobs? Well, they would have shut down the workshops and factories, even the whole city. Out in the streets they would stop the traffic, causing mayhem in the manner of the gilets jaunes in France. In these postmodern times, we do not think of popular mobilization in terms of organizational structures and leadership. It can be without a centre and organized through Facebook and Twitter, as the anthropologist-activist David Graeber has argued.[11] Postmodern political movement might even take a page from Elias Canetti's *Crowds and Power*.[12] Before we can speak of agendas, the target of struggle, we've got to have the numbers, the horde of people out in the street. Canetti writes:

> It is only in a crowd that man can become free of this fear of being touched. That is the only situation in which the fear changes into its opposite. The crowd he needs is the dense crowd, in which body is pressed to body; a crowd, too, whose psychical constitution is also dense, or compact, so that he no longer notices who it is that presses against him. As soon as a man has surrendered himself to the crowd, he ceases to fear its touch. Ideally, all are equal there; no distinctions count. Not even that of sex. The man pressed against him is the same as himself. He feels him as he feels himself. Suddenly it is as though everything were happening in one and the same body.[13]

It is the crowd—all equal, body pressed against body—that makes us see the wider significance of the shop assistants everywhere with their free-wheeling desires and sense of self-discovery.

Very few shopboys who had worked for us went back to the villages or townships where they came from. They appeared to have lost themselves in the city's gigantic maw that swallowed up everything. Visiting their parents, I got the vague answers. He is working in a furniture workshop now; hasn't he told you? Or: he told me he's got a new job in Ipoh, but I have not heard from him for months. Maybe the parents, practical people as they were, had let their sons be. The boy was making money; he was getting on with life and found his own way. Equally likely, I thought, the boys had found a new freedom, and the city life had made them reassess what their parents had planned for them. Maybe learning a trade and having their own shop was not all they wanted. After I got back from the university, I tried to find out what became of them. News came back in dribs and drabs, not all credible. I remember I was thrilled when one of the boys had gone to work in a used-car yard, or as a runner in a backyard betting shop or an enforcer for a loan shark. These were not the jobs their parents had in mind. But they paid well, and they had the rough and tumble that work at the High Street shop was not. The shopboys had rejected the genteel trades, which would have pleased the bellicose Wells had he known about them. To my mind, they had seen through the sham of the small family business and its civilized pretensions; the monastic dormitory had not damaged them or stunted their aspirations.

We called him Chew Tsai, 'Little Chew', who came from Kajang, outside Kuala Lumpur. The 'Little' of his nickname was ironic, for he was strongly built and heavily muscled. But his skin was smooth and fair, and his face a taut plumpness that gave him a blooming, feminine look. His eyes were alert when he spoke, even in a casual conversation—sign of a man quick to grasp at an issue and its importance. Among the shopboys, he alone had moved up the ladder from shop floor to sales counter. In his new position, his ripped singlets and pyjama pants had given way to white t-shirts and elegant dark trousers, and his natural scoffing to patient smile. He became a favourite of the lady customers who wanted to seek his advice, who wanted to know which type of ginseng would restore bodily vitality, which grade of pearls what would help to tone up the skin. However, his old taciturn air stayed with him. At the counter when business was down, he took on a faraway look—like a sea captain at the harbour waiting for fair weather.

I got to know Little Chew well because he was for a time my driving teacher. Over three months, every Sunday morning took me in the family Toyota to the Lake Gardens to practise driving at an empty car park. His manner of teaching was aggressive coaxing. Before handing over the wheel, he would recite the instructions: accelerator up; clutch down; changing gear—remember the drill. On a busy road don't panic and let others pass. He always seemed to be in a bad mood. I was grateful for the lessons, but a little afraid of him. After a brief turn around the narrow roads, we would turn to the car park where I was left to practise on my own. Thanks to him, I got my driver's licence. He had not charged me—how could he, he was 'one of the family'—yet I felt I had paid for the driving lessons by putting up with his grouchiness.

Chew Tsai's parents were fellow Hakka kin who ran a small herbalist-sundry store. In those days, a journey to Kajang still had an air of danger—not of guerrilla attacks since the Emergency had long ended, but of the 'crime wave' committed by young offenders. During one of our visits, my father and I had parked our car under a giant angsana tree near one of the back streets. We returned to find the wheels and tyres removed, an efficient gutting that left the car sitting on a few stumps of bricks. Chew Tsai's father sighed, then helped us to call the garage. As the mechanics went about their business, we waited and listened to Old Chew's rambling. The town, he said, had all but taken over by juvenile gangs—boys and a few girls with too much time on their hands—that caused havoc to the peaceful folks in town. Then came the request: please take Chew Tsai with you, find him something to do. I need to get him out. We never found out what the boy had actually done. It was enough that the boy needed rescuing, a place where he would be separated from the bad eggs. So we took him on to join the team of restless young boys in the shop.

He started with lowly jobs. He swept the floor; he helped to load and unload the vans and lorries; at night he shut and locked the iron accordion-door. Later he moved up to the toasting and grinding of herbs. At night at the dormitory he went through the rituals of humiliation like a new boy's ragging in an all-male boarding school. His heavily Brylcreemed hair was a subject of derision. His spectacular frugality was teased at when he darkened his white canvas shoes with boot polish to give them a glossy, black-leather look. But he put up with all this and bid his time. His final admittance was signalled by his joining the shop-floor comrades' endless bellyaching. He was skilful with words, and his sly expressions helped to coalesce what were on the young boys' minds. And he was soon the leader who marshalled the grumbling. Last year my bonus was three hundred ringgit—how much did you guys get? The business has been good this year, and the old man made a lot of money, but we get the same amount. You tell me: Is that fair? The docile small-town boy had turned recalcitrant.

When Chew Tsai was promoted to the sales counter, few were surprised. He was smart and quick to learn. He had a way with the customers, and he had made himself useful to the boss. Unlike the older workers, he kept his sneer and his habit of disparaging the boss to himself and among the shopboys. When told, my father would brush it aside: it was adolescent griping, and he had other things to think about. Besides, he rather remembered the young man's better qualities: he knew the prices of goods, and he had made the effort to remember the herbs inside each wooden cabinet set against the wall at the counter. And he had been borrowing the books and learning Chinese medicine. In my father's assessment, he was barely nineteen but he was the most talented, the most ambitious among the shopboys.

My father may have boasted about picking him up and getting him a job in the shop. But the fact was he soon became dependent on the young man. My father had wanted someone who could share his work, someone who knew the nitty-gritty of the herbal business. Besides my mother, there was no one else. At the time, my elder brother, having just finished his accountancy training, had begun working with IMB. He travelled a lot; he was trying to build his own career. And I was too young and too distracted. So my father took Chew Tsai under his wing, and a relationship of sort began to grow between them. People gossiped and sent out the idea my father had taken on a 'surrogate son'. But we shrugged our shoulders and let it go.

Chew Tsai was in all appearances a good salesperson. At the counter, he said: Oh, Madam, you have such good eye; only you know the genuine article from the faked ones, and: This is last set, honestly. These North Korean ginsengs don't come by often, and you know that. Later when my father started his mobile wholesale business, Chew Tsai was put in charge. Over two days in the weekend, we packed the VW combi van full of goods, and Chew Tsai would drive and deliver them directly to the retailers in the countryside. I often volunteered to go along. On those trips, in dealing with the shops, he was the 'little boss' who charmed and bargained, who cajoled and extracted payments when it was due. I felt he was rapidly learning the tricks. Serving his boss, he was also testing the waters: could he do this by himself—the oiling of the guanxi machine, the building of customer base, making the decision between concession and overcharging? And he seemed to have quietened down. The shopboys felt betrayed that he no longer led the nightly ranting and raving. As for working with the boss, he was gradually adopting an attitude of quiet accommodation and compromise.

It is a remarkable thing: he alone among the shopboys had made it. Thrust by his parents into the city, he saw the High Street shop as a stepping stone. He would learn a trade and better himself. In my father thinking, he was that rare one among the shopboys who had come and gone, one who had cracked the esoteric meanings of the medical texts and memorized the prescriptions. My father was sure young Chew would go far.

As if abiding by the script of the petty capitalist dream, less a decade later, he got married and opened a medicine shop in the middle-class suburb of Petaling Jaya next to the Asia Jaya supermarket. I looked him up as I went about closing the family shop. Sitting in his own shop, he had held on to his old faraway look. His words were unhurried, as though he was slowing down and directing my attention to his evident achievements.

He looked prosperous in his trademark Eagle-and-Tower brand t-shirt, presiding over the shop staffed by his siblings who had moved from Kajang to help run it. The shop was an air-conditioned mini-market. It dealt in herbs and patent medicine, but there were also shampoo and toiletries, brandy and whiskey and Benedictine. During festivals the shop offered gift baskets of canned fruits and liquor for customers to send their friends and associates.

During my first visit, I had thought: since my siblings and I were not interested, perhaps an arrangement could have been made that allowed Chew Tsai to take over the family shop. Father had trained him, and he would have made it a success more than any of us could. And the family legacy would be secured.

Chinese petite capitalism prides itself as the 'capitalism of the little person'. Anyone could start a small shop or stall. A man or a woman with modest savings could become a street peddler, a hawker, a stall keeper in the night market. The term rolls smoothly off the tongue: zuo xiao sheng yi, making a small living. The 'smallness' of the undertaking suggests an 'any one can do it' equalitarianism. And it dares the salary earner: give up your miserable wage and work for yourself. This had been my father's wisdom: a worker who stays an employee reveals a lack of character, and worker who has saved up to start his own business is a mercantile hero. He thought working for others to be subservient and enfeebling. The transformation from employee to shop owner is a leap of destiny. It gives you self-respect and defines you as a person. The fact not all shop workers become shop owners merely reinforces the need for personal drive and initiative. Petite capitalism may be little in capital and in the size of trade, but it is big in dreams and ambitions.

Chew Tsai's rise is a perfect fit with this narrative. My father had picked him up from the grimy shop floor because he saw in the young man the drive and initiative he once saw in himself. He might even see Chew Tsai's grouchiness as a sign of independence and single-mindedness, qualities necessary to make good in the business world. In my thinking, it is certain that he had been socialized into the values that my father had held dear, and that the experience at the shop had moulded him into what he was.

The shopboys who went through the High Street shop were like winged-seeds that have taken roots not far off from the mother plant. Each time I saw them—in the car park washing and waxing cars, helping in the night market selling packed herbal mixtures and sundry goods, in the coffee shop waiting on customers as disgruntled as they—they were not strangers to me. I didn't go over to talk to them, but I was happy that they had found a footing in the city. Their jobs might not have counted for much, but at least they didn't return to the miserable life back home they had complained about, or to work at another medicine shop; that was achievement enough. Their experience in the High Street shop was tough, unpampered, and they had seen through the face of power and paternalism. They had a sense of who they truly were. It would be foolish to leave the shop, but it would more so to have stayed. The realization must have travelled with them to wherever they went. They were different persons from what had been when they started at the High Street shop. And I had a feeling that they were not fooled by their new bosses who deployed the same tricks of benevolence, the same subtle concealment of power and intentions. One or two might even have joined the labour union or the opposition parties as a frontline soldier of change. After all, one of them, my Second Cousin who stayed with us for a couple of years, had joined the communist insurgents and got killed.[14] The shopboys, feet dug deep in the city, came across as stout-hearted with a touch of valour.

My parents had kept in touch with Chew Tsai after he left. I suppose they liked him. Chew Tsai's mini-mart near the Asia Supermarket was evidence of what hard work and persistence could achieve. But I saw it with a different eye each time I visited the place. It reminded me of the High Street shop. Take way the Panasonic air-curtain, the steel shelving, the health products, it was the same place of petite capitalism, the same reverie of profit and profit-making. And Chew Tsai resting on the low chair, with his darkened hair and thick neck, made me think of those famous pictures of Mao in his later years, soft, paunchy, short of the rigour of his younger years. As for my 'shop-floor heroes': what would they think of him? I wonder. Some would perhaps envy him. But some, I am sure, would smell the scent of betrayal. Some might even think: He alone had made it, and that made him an 'enemy': one of those whom they had raged against at night in the dormitory at the High Street shop.

I began to walk out from the mini-mart and it felt like freedom.

## Notes

1. Antonio Gramsci, 'Some aspects of the southern question'. In *Selections from political writings (1921–1926)*, Translated and edited by Quintin Hoare. London: Lawrence and Wishart, 1978. Michel Foucault. *Discipline and Punish.* Translated by Alan Sheridan. NY: Vintage Books, 2012.

2. Oscar Wilde, 'The Soul of Man Under Socialism' In *Complete Works of Oscar Wilde*, edited by Vyvyan Holland, London: Collins, 1969, p. 1081
3. Ibid.
4. Goffman, Erving. *Asylums: Essays on the Social Situation of Mental Patients and Other Inmates.* NY: Anchor Books, 1961. Foucault, Michel. *Discipline and Punish.* Translated by Alan Sheridan. NY: Vintage Books, 2012.
5. Christopher P Hosgood, '"Mercantile Monasteries": Shops, Shop Assistants, and Shop Life in Late-Victorian and Edwardian Britain'. *J. Br. Stud.* 38 (3), 1999, p. 325.
6. Ibid., pp. 331–332.
7. Ibid., p. 336
8. Ibid., p. 331.
9. Wells, H. G., *Experiment in Autobiography.* London: Faber & Faber, 2011, p. 149.
10. Ibid., p. 150.
11. David Graeber, *The Democracy Project: A History, a Crisis, a Movement.* NY: Spiegel & Grau, 2013.
12. Elias Canetti, *Crowds and Power.* Edited and translated by Carol Stewart. New York: Viking Press, 1962.
13. Ibid., p. 15.
14. See my: *The Malayan Emergency: Essays on a Small, Distant War*, Copenhagen: NIAS Press, 2016, chapter 9.

## Bibliography

Canetti, Elias. 1962. *Crowds and Power.* Edited and translated by Carol Stewart. New York: Viking Press.

Foucault, Michel. 2012. *Discipline and Punish.* Translated by Alan Sheridan. NY: Vintage Books.

Goffman, Erving. 1961. *Asylums: Essays on the Social Situation of Mental Patients and Other Inmates.* NY: Anchor Books.

Graeber, David. 2013. *The Democracy Project: A History, A Crisis, a Movement.* NY: Spiegel & Grau.

Gramsci, Antonio. 1978. 'Some aspects of the southern question'. In *Selections from political writings (1921–1926).* Translated and edited by Quintin Hoare. London: Lawrence and Wishart.

Hosgood, Christopher P. 1999. '"Mercantile Monasteries": Shops, Shop Assistants, and Shop Life in Late-Victorian and Edwardian Britain'. *J. Br. Stud.* 38 (3): 322–352.

Wells, H. G. 2011. *Experiment in Autobiography.* London: Faber & Faber.

Wilde, Oscar. 1969. 'The Soul of Man Under Socialism'. In *Complete Works of Oscar Wilde.* Edited by Vyvyan Holland, London: Collins.

Yao, Souchou. *The Malayan Emergency: Essays on a Small, Distant War*, Copenhagen: NIAS Press, 2016.

CHAPTER 6

# Tiger Parenting

Education is a major part of the story of Chinese petite capitalism; it is also the story of the Chinese diaspora generally. I do not speak for other ethnic communities, but in Southeast Asia, the Chinese have a reputation for investing heavily in their children's education. It is something people in the region have very much come to acknowledge. Like all social facts, this too is subject to interpretation and nitpicking by all manner of people. In Malaysia, many see a near obsession with education as the secret of the success of the ethnic Chinese. For the ethnic Chinese themselves, their social and economic achievements are a source of pride, though you learn to underplay them lest they incite resentment from others. Between the resentment and ethnic pride lie many shades of truth and understanding. Nothing is immune from the fervour of ethnic politics. Malaysia is proud of its formula for ethnic peace: a mixture of positive discrimination for some, lowering of expectations for others and the sharing of state power and privileges between the community elites. The formula has more or less worked. The average Malaysian family, like ours, is neither endowed with inheritance and wealth nor the connections with powerful people. And we are right to feel bitter. The state grants and scholarships favour the Malays, and the local universities limit the enrolment for non-Malay students, and not every parent can afford the expensive of private universities.[1] In any event, education—and the ethnic discrimination that drives it—make for a sorry affair for *all* communities. Those who have been left out feel done in, and forever injured by a sense of injustice. And those who have benefited



S. Yao, *The Shop on High Street*,
https://doi.org/10.1007/978-981-15-2031-0_6

have their burden too. They have come through the state system and bear the sigma of those deemed less talented, and the more sensitive among them resent the judgement that they have not gained their positions by their own merit.

This is a yarn of many strands, and we are only speaking of tertiary education. Everyone complains, so it seems, including those at whom the state assistance is targeted. To my family's credit, we never went in for blaming the government or the Malay community for our lack of opportunities. It was lame political consciousness; it was also realism—the realization that government scholarships were not for the likes of us. And it was also the classic petty bourgeoise sensibility. Faced with the problem, we felt there was no help we could have except from ourselves. There was no heroism in this, except the trying circumstances and a lot of creative budgeting by my father. I think back, and my young self was like the Chinese boy Robert, a musical wunderkind, in Anthony Burgess' *The Malayan Trilogy*.[2] We did not want to follow in our parents' footsteps and become shopkeepers. Robert has the ambition of writing symphonies, and I had wanted to go to university. For him it is 'from the Chinese shophouse to the Carnegie Hall' (if he gets his US-government grant), and I had a vague idea of becoming an economist. Forced by the state ethnic politics at home, I was sent away and the foreign sojourn had been an achievement for me and for my shopkeeper parents. If this is a successful story, it is also one of homesickness and fear: fear of failing in the exams, fear of disappointing my parents. I may indeed protest too much; after all I had made it and returned in triumph. Yet to rework Tolstoy: families with successful children are all alike; every family with less successful children is on its own. For a variety of reasons some children fail to perform and acquire a medical or engineering or law degree. It is a great tragedy when this happens. Children who don't measure up bring trouble to the family; they abort the carefully chiselled plan of their parents, a plan that has little tolerance for mishaps and change of directions half way towards the destination.

Still, not all Chinese parents are rampant materialists. I know my parents wanted us to graduate and have well-paid professional jobs. And they also wanted us to be decent and ethical-minded, and that meant we would come back from the university with more than a degree. We were brought up by tiger parents before the term was invented, and it is easy to list what they were expected of us: hardworking and disciplined, a secure job to support ourselves and our parents in their old age, and devotion to the family. The family was to our parents a cultural fixation. They had in mind that for the children the few years of university overseas was a temporary sojourn, after which they would return home and carry on as before. It has always been a bit of shocking realization to me that parents could send their children away and believe they would pick up the life from where they had left it.

Yet so much is stacked against this notion of the family and all it represents. I can, Rousseau-like, speak of education's powerful liberating experience. Each time I think about it, something else intrudes on the scene of blissful pursuits and romantic self-realization. For I knew that I had been sent to the university not only for myself, but also for the family. And this is the irony: university education makes one disloyal and defiant of what the parents had planned. My father thought university was a lasting gift for his children, a safe bid to secure a good and profitable career. But it also nurtured in us a sense ambivalence about his values and way of life, which we were ready to renounce when we returned.

Perhaps it is too easy to blame it on education. The desire to live one's life, the need to break out from the family: where did these feelings come from? You scan the depth of your memory and find it hard to know where to begin. When, at what moment, was one's first inkling of unsettling? Perhaps it was the Hollywood cinema with its stoic handsome men and impossibly glamorous women. Or probably it was the Beatles or Eric Clapton whose music shamed the shrill sing-song of Peking Opera my parents liked. Most likely, the feeling of alienation came to you when you first felt the narrow horizon of your parents' vision. But then who would blame them, for they had all their life worked in a shophouse that made them tight-fisted and pragmatic. Still, you felt guilty for your judgement. You wanted to be fair, because they had loved you and sacrificed a great deal for you. When the shop was being closed down, the relatives tried to pin the blame on us—on our over-spending the family money, for staying away when we should be at home helping to run the business. They seemed like platitudes. Yet they left me with the thought: against the love and security, family is but a set of responsibilities, a jumble of obligations. It is not easy to strike a balance between the need to shoulder these responsibilities and obligations, and the desire to strike out on one's own.

The idea of tiger parenting is actually several ideas in one. It is an expression of ethnic pride; it counsels that tough, knuckle-down discipline of the children will ensure their economic future; it is an Orientalist fantasy; it decries the 'Western educational model' of individual fulfilment and self-realization; it is the time-proven Chinese—East Asian—way of bringing up children. My parents, though they didn't know the term tiger parenting, practised a version of it. The idea has been around for a while, but it was Amy Chua's 2011 bestseller *Battle Hymn of the Tiger Mother* that has helped it to gain great popularity.[3] *Battle Hymn* is a high readable book, full of vignettes of Chua's family life and of her two young daughters coping with school and their growing-up issues. Chua insists that *Battle Hymn* is not a manual for how to bring up one's children. The defence, however, is not helped by some of her assertions.

> There are all kinds of psychological disorders in the West that don't exist in Asia. The fact is that Chinese parents can do things that would seem unimaginable – even legally actionable – to Westerners. Chinese mothers can say to their daughters, 'Hey fatty – lose some weight.' By contrast, Western parents have to tiptoe around the issue, talking in terms of 'health' and never ever mentioning the f-word, and their kids still end up in therapy for eating disorders and negative self image.

And she brings up the common misunderstanding of the Chinese childrearing:

> Once when I was young – maybe more than once – when I was extremely disrespectful to my mother, my father angrily called me "garbage" in our native Hokkien dialect. It worked really well. I felt terrible and deeply ashamed of what I had done. But it didn't damage my self esteem or anything like that. I knew exactly how highly he thought of me. I didn't actually think I was worthless or feel like a piece of garbage. As an adult, I once did the same thing to Sophie, calling her garbage in English when she acted extremely disrespectful toward me. When I mentioned I had done this at a dinner party, I was immediately ostracized. One guest named Marcy got so upset she broke down in tears and had to leave early.

My parents were not such strict disciplinarians; neither I nor my siblings had the benefits of being called 'garbage' in the way of bolstering our self-esteem. Sleepovers, piano lessons and cheerleaders were not our world. About *Battle Hymn*, I can go on and on about the Orientalist fantasy—the Lacanian othering of Asian model minorities in order to make a grab for their time-honoured method of childrearing. But this is not quite the right approach. To subject *Battle Hymn* to philosophic scrutiny is overkill, a warped theoretical treatment.

The trouble is there is much in a Chinese upbringing—if less in Amy Chua's depiction of it—that one finds appealing. I mean, what is there not to like with an upbringing that is full of love and moral teaching, with an occasional 'we know what is good for you' disciplining? And then: isn't our 'from shophouse to university' mobility an undisputable evidence of the wisdom of tiger parenting? But this is simplifying a great deal. We have indeed succeeded, but there were times when success didn't seem assured, when tiger parenting came across as less than infallible. There were obstacles and there were lucky breaks, and it's hard to know which would eventually win out. We had lived through the grind of tiger parenting, but it could not keep at bay the outside influences and experiences. They had changed us, and they had worked against the attempt to turn us into young adults in our parents' mould.

The story of my education began with the British colonial legacy in which the English schools enjoyed a special position. In the British times—and for some years after independence—to have a child in an English school was a source of pride for the parents; finishing in an English school more or less guaranteed a job in the civil service and in the Western multinational firms. Certainly an English education was the only way to matriculate and enter a local or overseas university. The English schools had tell-tale names: Victoria Institution, Raffles Institution (in Singapore), Methodist Boys' School, Methodist Girls' School, Bukit Nanas Convent School and the various Anglo-Chinese Schools across the peninsula. Run by churches, their pedagogic aim was to turn out young men and women of Christian and pro-British liberal views. The colony even had a Malayan Eton, the Kuala Kangsar College, which admitted, and still does, children of the Malay elite. The British had made the education system a part of the policy of divide and rule. Besides the English schools there were the schools taught in Chinese or in Tamil. Speaking of the Chinese schools, they enjoyed no official patronage. They were funded by the community whose members, rich and poor alike, regarded education with near reverence. This, together with the Chinese talent for self-help, enabled the Chinese schools to enjoy a large degree of independence; they were left to decide on the curriculum, the recruitment of teachers and how the schools were managed. After Independence in 1957, the cry was national integration. The education reforms turned the English schools into so-called national-type schools, with full state funding and Malay as the language of instruction and the teaching of state curriculum. All primary schools were national-type schools. Those secondary schools that opted out of the state system became independent schools; they received no state assistance and relied on community funding as in the old days.

This briefly is the origin of the two-tiered school system found in Malaysia today. The Chinese independent school tells a fascinating story of British colonialism, the ethnic politics of the postcolonial state, the struggle for cultural and educational rights and the elite competition for the leadership of the Chinese education movement.[4] It is a subject that affects many parents today in deciding where to send their children for schooling.

My siblings and I went to Chinese independent schools; mine was the improbably named Confucius Chinese Middle School founded in 1906 and located in the Petaling Street neighbourhood in the city. It has since heavily renovated, but during my time the school was a ramshackle three-story building, each floor open to the verandah. A gigantic ficus tree dominated the school yard at the front, providing shade during the school assembly, but its roots were eating into the ground and onto the monsoon drain. The ficus tree, the mould-darkened walls, the parasite plants sprouting from the building's nooks and crannies—they gave the building the look of an ancient ruin. However, we were unfazed. The look was for us not a sign of neglect, but an evidence of the austerity and money-saving that had ensured the school's survival. The school board could not, we were sure, spend money on white washing the building each year when substantial donation had come from the hawkers and labourers and shopkeepers in the community. A major renovation could not be justified. Besides, there were other ways to spend the money—the science laboratory, the stationary supplies, the classroom furniture, the teachers' salaries. As we stood in school assembly under the morning sun, we felt an enormous sense of pride. We owed our education to public charity; paved footpath and well-clipped lawns and hedges, not to say a football field, were not for us. So the school kept its faded architectural glory, like some Dickensian dowager with her old wedding dress.

I remember the school's spartan architecture and what we were taught. We were children of hawkers and petty traders and shopkeepers. We were to be tutored on the cultural heritage of the ancestral country, with concessions to modern thinking and the demands of the nation-state of which we were citizens. The pedagogic aims were baroque and not easily reconciled with each other. In history lessons, we were taught about Malaya under the British, with a brief excursion to the Buddhist Srivijaya Empire between the seventh and thirteenth centuries, followed by the Hindu Majapahit Empire and the Portuguese and Dutch presence in the peninsula. We had one-hour daily class of Bahasa Kebangsan, Malay the national language. On the whole, there was a good deal of business as usual in the curriculum. English classes were taught by the affable Miss Lim, with a heavy emphasis on grammar—the tenses, the difference between a phrase and a clause, between transitive and intransitive verbs. And we were made to read excerpts from Kipling, Stevenson, Sir Walter Scott and Richard Blackmore's *Lorna Doone* in the Longman Simplified English Series. Apart from the Malay and English classes, teaching remained more or less China-focused. We learnt by heart the geography of the Chinese provinces, and we read passages from Sima Qian's monumental Record of History that chronicled the soapy courtly intrigues and the changes of dynasties. The Chinese literature class was two hours a day. At senior middle three—third-year high school—we moved to an anthology of selected readings of the ancient texts: Confucius Analects, Dao De Qing, the poetry of the Sung and Tang period. It gave us a solid grounding in classical Chinese. By the time we got to the Qing literature of Hong Lou Meng, Dream of the Red Chamber and Shen Fu's Six Records of a Floating Life, they didn't seem daunting to us. The anthology we used in the literature class also included the modern voices. There were passages of novels and essays from the May Fourth movement of 1919: Lu Xun's A Madman's Diary, Ba Jin's Family, Spring, Autumn Trilogy, Ding Ling's Miss Sophia's Diary. And then there was European and American literature in translation—selected passages from the works of Mark Twain, Stevenson, Jack London, some Conrad.

It was a mish-mash of a pedagogic experience, powerful and memorable. As I have described elsewhere:

> Educated in the Confucius Chinese Middle School in Kuala Lumpur in the 1960s, I remember my engagement with Chinese literary works as both complex and absorbing. The teaching of literature had been singularly designed to socialise us in the literary and ethical worth of classical texts. For three hours a day, we read, copied and took dictation from an anthology consisting of excerpts from basic works ranging from the philosophic writings of Mencius and Confucius to the poetry of Li Po and Su Dong Po, as well as the modern works of Lu Xun, Ding Ling and Ba Jin. Brush calligraphy was an important part of our daily Chinese language class, in which I acquired sufficient skill to win the All Chinese Medium School championship. For most of us, moving between the classical philosophic texts and the vernacular modernist voices of Lu Xun and Ding Ling seemed most natural. They were all a part of the 'Chinese cultural heritage'. Through these texts, and art forms like brush calligraphy, we acquired a sense of 'knowing China'.

> It was a sense of having a certain access to her tradition, culture and national aspirations which through some tortuous ways were made a part of ourselves.[5]

Our reading moved naturally from one literary form to another, from Chinese texts to the texts of Western origin. Our teacher, the long-suffering Mr Chang, taught his class with wary circumspection. He made plain for us the abstruse poetics and arcane expressions of classic Chinese, and he was determined to get across the message from the texts. Through both the English and Chinese classes, the rise and fall of dynasties; the folly of Ah Q, the Chinese Everyman in Lu Xun's classic novel; the young captain in Conrad's *The Secret Sharer*: they were lessons on human frailty and moral resolve, told from different perspectives. So we were taught.

What else happened at school—besides reading and writing and struggling with the diverse texts? I like to believe I did the truancy, the occasional cheating in exams, the schoolyard fights that all teenagers of my age did. But these do not stand out in my memory. Still, you have to remember what anxious parents I had and their values. And is it boasting when I relate that after school I did nothing else but help in the shop? It was simply the Chinese petite capitalist existence. As for tiger parenting, my parents were too busy to micromanage our schoolwork so they let us get on with it. We were freer; we enjoyed greater liberty than the children in Amy Chua's household. The truth is that we were brought up with a kind of division of labour: our parents made the money; we children looked after our own schooling, more or less. The approach had provided space and privacy that Chua's daughters would have envied. Our family life was tight and disciplined, but it was not suffocating. There were opportunities to test the ground and channel our rebelliousness.

A last note on *Battle Hymn*: Professor Chua's children have an education many could only dream about. Migrants and refugees have fought to enter the United States, and securing their children's future is a big part of it. To get a slice of the American dream, however, good grades and parental pressure are not the only essential factors. Wealth and class privileges are important too. And wealth and class privileges mean socializing the children in a certain way. They are pampered; they are made to feel a sense of entitlement; their wild self-searching is nipped at the bud. The wayward children of tiger parents are hauled screaming and kicking onto the right path. As regards to what Chua has in mind for her daughters, one asks an outsider's question. Why is the American school system so monolithically conformist in the way she describes it? Surely in the elite school her children go to, some pupils aspire to be rock stars or ballet dancers or chefs or school supervisors? Jobs of honest labour, and no one can say they are less worthy, less socially useful, than a Harvard law professorship.

For all I have said about my parents, it is true that at the back of their minds they did not want their children to live the life as they had. They put a high premium on education and familial loyalty, but they also foresaw a life for the children different from theirs. The best outcome for them was, with our professional job, we would after graduation stay and work in Malaysia. It was a best compromise between a foreign education and the home-bound virtue. Sending us to a Chinese school was to make us remember our cultural roots, and to free us from the Anglophilia common among the educated. Everything was about striking a balance—between Chinese learning and foreign learning, between individual needs and obligations to the family.

Chinese—or more broadly, East Asian—young people are not very good at winning the Oedipal struggle. It is an uphill battle when parental demands are delivered by hands in the velvet gloves of love and reconciliation. Often the battle is lost even before it has begun. In any case, there is little to fight over when you and your parents share the same aspirations; when you, too, wanted social status and a secure high-salaried professional job. So the need for self-realization is a compromise. You love your parents, and you seek opportunities to escape their authority and influence. And sometimes opportunities come to you in surprising ways. You take your life-forming experiences where you can get them.

Sending me to university in Australia was my parents' big investment in their third son. We'll get the money, they said, you just worry about your studies. I was an eighteen-year-old from tropical Asia, and I was going alone to a foreign country. We children from Chinese shophouses did not speak of homesickness and the coping mechanism, but we faced the fact of our poor English. At the Confucius Middle School, the English classes never gave us skills beyond elementary reading and writing. Miss Lim did us no favour by failing to control the class, and the Longman Simplified English Series was infantile stuff. One who wished to go overseas would need to raise the English language competence. This meant finding a private tutor, and fortunately good accomplished English tutors were not hard to come by.

Dr Raju, PhD, University of Calcutta, was a retired school principal. My father approved of Indian teachers because they could speak English the way a Chinese person could not; they could speak fast and roll their 'R's' and get the words right. We asked around and people had vouched for Dr Raju with his nearly forty years of teaching career, now retired. We got his phone number and made an appointment. One night, my father and I loaded half a dozen bottles of Remy Martin—a cash gift would be too crude—into the car and drove to his house. He was standing at the door when we came up the driveway. We went in and followed him to his study: a big writing desk, a tall shelf full of books and papers, a coffee table covered with golf magazines. Mrs Raju came in with a tray and served us tea, then left us. We did small talks and introduced ourselves. Dr Raju eyed me over and said:

> Okay, I'll teach you. I heard you Chinese students are all work and no play. That's fine with me. I'll make you work. He then turned to my father: Okay, I'll take him on. Leave him with me.

I went to his house two nights a week, from six to nine. He got me to read aloud passages from Thomas Hardy's *Far from the Madding Crowd*, Wilkie Collins' *The Woman in White*, Dickens' *A Tale of Two Cities*. As I read, he would pat his right hand on the table and said:

> You've got to spread the consonants, you must make each sound distinct like a drum beat. Like this: thump, thump, thump, thump. And don't swallow the vowels! he would add and do a mock beating on my heads with a ruler. You don't speak the street English in my house.

We also did a lot of grammar drills: how to change a phrase into a clause; how to differentiate a conditional clause from an adjectival clause, a past tense from past participle. He was a good teacher, a bit of a disciplinarian. And he made me feel that each mispronunciation, each wrong sentence construction was a betrayal of the language of a great civilization. I learnt a great deal from the endearing old man.

The week before I left for Adelaide I went back to his house to say goodbye. In the study filled with evening's last light, Dr Raju and his wife sat with me to talk. Mrs Raju had placed the tea pot before me: It's masala chai, spicy the way you like it. She asked about my parents, and if I was looking forward to leaving, then she left us to ourselves. We began to talk, and something happened that had the feel of an omen. Dr Raju was sitting behind the desk and holding a glass of cognac in his hand. As he stood up, he knocked the pencil box off the table. Don't worry, let Mrs Raju do it, he said quickly. But I would not have it. I bent down and picked up the pencils and chalk pieces from the floor and put them back to the pencil box. I felt the need, I don't know why, to fuss over him, to help him when he couldn't help himself. He was old, he was tipsy as he tried to get up from the chair. Neither Mrs Raju nor I could blame him for the little misadventure. He was my teacher, and he had offered up a whole vista of things so excitingly different from what my sing-song native tongue could describe.

I told him about my journey. I told him that I was to do an economics degree and come back to work in a bank. It was a plan I had worked out with my father, I explained. He jerked his shoulders and looked at me with his grave, dark eyes. Work hard and don't waste your father's money, he said. Your father has sacrificed a lot for you. Remember what I taught you, and make something of yourself.

The words didn't then sound like the clichés that they do now. 'Make something of yourself': I knew he meant being an adult, one who is responsible and grateful to his or her parents. And he assured me what lay ahead in the foreign land was worth leaving home for. In any case, that was the last time I saw him. A year later, in Adelaide, I received a letter from Mrs Raju. She wrote to tell me that her husband had died peacefully in his sleep, which made me regret I had not kept in touch, that I had not written to one who had mattered a good deal to my young life.

Roland Barthes speaks of eating in a dining car of the French railway; it 'was not so much food as a philosophy', it was a 'mirage of solidity' as the shuttling scene at the window reminded you everything was in motion Barthes (1979). Eating on the train was both orderly and 'on the move'—the experience came to you in strange waves of sensations. At the end, the wine did not spill and you had somehow dined elegantly (Ibid). I rather think life-forming experiences are like eating on a French railway diner. The experiences are strange yet orderly; they are unpredictable yet you can trace their origin and the effects they have had on you. As my mind moves from the family to the shophouse, from the Confucius Middle School to the university, these events had their own momentum; yet they did not appear random or arbitrary. They had a history and a social and practical reason. And they featured charming serendipities—and the blessings of strangers like Dr Raju. The legacies they left were solid yet mysterious. If the Chinese school and Mr Raju had left their mark, what about Madam Le Clair my pen pal who sent me stamps from Paris? For a young teen growing up in Southeast Asia, the truly parochialism-busting experience might well be the cinema. How could one forget the wet embrace of Burt

Lancaster and Deborah Kerr on the beach after a midnight swim in *From Here to Eternity*, their bodies spreading across the Cinemascope screen at the local movie theatre? If the life-forming experiences are stable yet incidental, what strikes me most was their overwrought sensuality. They were life-forming because they were powerful and unforgettable, because they made you dizzy with amazement as they carved your senses into the beginning of a recognition, an individual identity.

Or take the British Council library.

The British Council Library sat on a hill that looked down on the busy Jalan Raja in the city. The height and white-washed gleam gave the building the majestic look of a watchtower by the sea. You ducked through the traffic and crossed the road, and with your heavy school bag, you began to make your climb, panting at every step, the concrete stairways eating into your white canvas shoes. It was hot, and the ascent made you feel like some pilgrim making her way to the temple at the mountain top. You reached the top and were met by a clipped green lawn with the hedge swinging its league along a stone-wall overlooking the road below. It was all green lawn and low hedges and horticultural sense for the library.

My friends and I used to come here looking for a place to study. Then they found the US-government Lincoln Cultural Centre down the hill near the Selangor River, and left me. On my own I chose a spot among the stacks away from the intimidating eyes of the Indian lady at the reference desk. I was surrounded by tomes after tomes of novels and philosophic tracts and reference books. The Oxford English Dictionary, works of the greats from Shakespeare to Samuel Johnson, Forster to Lawrence, and light entertainments from A J Cronin to Agatha Christie: they were all there. Remembering Dr Raju, I am tempted to say I was soaking up the atmosphere, swimming in the spirit of English literature. After my homework, I would walk along the rows and rows of books. The novels and essays and the Commonwealth University Year Book were the nearest thing to actually travelling in a foreign country. I was coasting among the great heavy tomes, my head filled with wonder.

I see I am already exaggerating. I knew little English at the time, so all this was a bit of fantasy. When I say I was soaking up British literature's great influence, it is truer to say I had gone to the library for the peace and quiet, with the librarians going about their business with unhurried efficiency. The place was everything the High Street shop was not. Going to the library was going to a strange, alien place whose meaning and purposes were vastly different from those of the dusty shop. The temple on the hill beamed 'come hither' to its worshippers, and I had answered its call. And this might have been more to do with the Carrier Air-conditioning than with the books and their mystery and aura.

One cannot tell one's growing-up story without telling one's discoveries outside the family. Among other things, tiger parenting is a pitch against the powerful allure of the world that tends to lead the children astray. So much lies outside of the family: friendships, pleasures of various sorts, jobs better paid and perhaps more congenial than ones offered by the family, and as the anthropologist would remind you, carnal desires and marital partners beyond the bounds of incest. Disloyalty—and alienation—are the family secrets tiger parenting is not too keen to tell.

In Adelaide, in the first months after I arrived, homesickness had struck me like pain. For all my fantasies about the land Down Under, I was not prepared for the grilled lamb chops and sardine sandwiches and weak milky tea Mrs Carter the landlady had prepared for this rice eater from the tropics. My room was at the back facing the garden through the door, and after the lectures I would return here and spend my time moping about, missing home and the family. To Mrs Carter and her church-going friends, I was a 'nice Asian student', polite and unassuming. To tell her of my misery would be unbecoming, a betrayal of her hospitality. In a moment of weakness, I wrote to my father saying how lonely I was. His reply was curt, to the point: If you don't like it there you can come back and join the shopboys stitching gunnysacks. It was a wakeup call; I needed to stop feeling sorry for myself. My remorse and my father's anger turned me around. I remember the exact moment when I decided *this* was now home. In that afternoon in Mrs Carter's house, it came to me that the bad food, the friendly but unfamiliar people, the students' aggressive show-off in tutorials, the panic attacks—they were realities I had to learn to accept. I put away my father's letter and walked out of the boarding house to the Curzon theatre a block away on Goodwood Road. I had been inside and seen the European films with subtitles, but I had yet learnt that they were films of Italian Neo-Realism and the French New Wave. The night's showing was Michelangelo Antonioni's *La Notte*. Jeanne Moreau's wandering in the Milan street at night, the male night creatures shooting glances from the dark laneway, seemed resonate with something deep inside me. Deborah Kerr on the beach had given place to Jeanne Moreau at night in Milan, or Jean Seberg in Parisian streets. Watching these films was a mixed sensation of eroticism, urban ennui, unique expressions of personal style and feelings. They were thrilling and invigorating, and they had nothing to do with the family at home. I was later to move out from Mrs Carter's house, but I returned, often with a friend, almost weekly to the Curzon Cinema.

Education was for my parents an extravagant idea. Education is precious; it is worthwhile to loosen one's wallet for; it ensures the children's future; it would free them from the miserable shophouse existence. These were our parents' gifts to us. They wanted for us a less stressful life, and better and more profitable jobs than theirs. And this was to be realized through the earnings of the High Street shop.

The Asian shophouse married work life and home life. It was a place of work and it was a place of emotional intimacy. We shared the happiness and triumph, and we shared the stress and each other's despair. And on a bad day when the take at the cash register was low, when things at the shop did not go smoothly, the ethos of sharing was like a pup tent after a storm: you were tangled up, you were strapped inside a place you didn't want to be in. The panic was overwhelming. With some exaggeration, I say I took this panic with me when I left home. The panic was of a different nature: the fear of failure in the exams, the fear of wasting my parents' money, the fear that I would not measure up to what they had expected of me. Of course, there were the rewards and excitement too. When I won the first prize in a university essay competition, it felt like a tribute to my parents and the values they had instilled in me. And after my father died, when I got a job at a chopsuey joint in Adelaide to support myself, I was acting as my father would have liked me to act: diligent, financially sensible, conscientious; and I hoped he would be pleased with me. A decade on, getting a university post in Singapore after months of looking seemed like an attempt to please him and seek his approval.

So in a way, my siblings and I have fulfilled what our parents had wanted for us. We had a good education, nearly all of us became professionals—an accountant, a pharmacist, a quantitative surveyor, an economist-turned-anthropologist. But we have also dismissed the family legacy—none wanted to take over the High Street shop business. We are free, and the shop should be put down like a tired old mule past its usefulness. We have branched out and we have become our own selves due to our own efforts, so we believe.

Over the years, conference gigs and lecture invitations have enabled me to stop over and visit my family in Malaysia. Father's death and the closure of the High Street shop have brought us closer; left to ourselves we've become more tolerant of each other's habits and career choices. My mother had lived for more than a decade after her husband's death, and while alive she was the focus of our affection. We made her comfortable as she stayed with my younger brother Paul. We had in mind that we should help her to make up for her lost years in working at the shop. She once came to visit me in Adelaide. I was in my pathetic post-doc year, living in a rented house and on a part-time lectureship that supported a family of three; and I forever regret I was not more filial, that I was unable to entertain her more lavishly. But as we talked, she had said: I don't care about dinners and gifts; I only want to see that you are well. Later, when I was fully tenured—Singapore, then Sydney—I would stop over in Kuala Lumpur and stay a few days. The homecoming, such as it was, made us sick with sentiment and misgiving. As we sat in the verandah of my younger brother Paul's house, I didn't know what to say half of the time; but for my mother it was always, You are working in a university now, how I wish your father was alive to see it.

There would be a reunion dinner and we would all go to the Paramount Seafood Restaurant in a shopping mall nearby. As we chew on boiled peanuts and waited for the dishes to arrive, there was lot of talk and exchange of news, ending with Paul's aggressive teasing: See, your favourite son is back; you should be happy now. Still, we were all here, Paul and I, my younger sister and her husband, the in-laws, the grandchildren, sitting around the table, our mother beaming with pride—only missing was our father and our second sister.

Paramount Seafood Restaurant was famous for its Shanghai mud crab and fresh lobster braced in wine sauce, and we plied our chopsticks in the dishes when they came one after another. My father and I always had fresh lobster in wine sauce when we had our father-and-son talks; so the dish was a memorial of sort. We had come to an expensive place, and we had ordered seafood; the bill was not going to be for the faint-hearted. But we could well afford the dinner, and no one was going to begrudge the expenses of celebrating my homecoming, and making our mother happy. We took our time with the dishes; we drank our tea and nibbled on the duty-free Swiss chocolate I'd brought back; we dragged on the hours. The waiter came with the bill, and without thinking we would begin to fight over it. Aggressive hands would reach out: No, no, let me do this. I can put it in the card, as if Visa or American Express were free cash, a mere piece of plastic. More often than not, I lost in the scramble. I was not fast enough, I was not skilled in the battle of generosity. The few times I excelled and won, the privilege of paying lifted my spirit and I felt gratified.

You see, I needed more than my siblings to make a splash, to demonstrate to the family that I, too, had made it. It was my secret. We have all succeeded in accordance to the script, yet stalking my mind was the feeling that I could have done better, that I could have taken up a profession more straightforwardly rewarding financially, more ostensibly of face and social status. The over-ambition of tiger parenting has left its mark. Even among its beneficiaries, tiger parenting grades them and picks its favourites. Had I stayed in the bank and persisted in the job at the foreign currency desk I would have been more like my siblings, and my achievement would have matched theirs. Do my siblings actually judge me so? I am sure they do not; it is only my self-consciousness. It makes me cringe as I write: my flashing of the gold premium HSBC Visa card at the restaurant counter, the casual mentioning of the new kitchen renovation and fresh bathroom makeover of our Sydney house, the talk of the few bluechip shares that I have just bought. These are gestures that normalize my existence, that make me like my siblings who have more correctly followed the script.

Tiger parenting cuts deep, its effects pathetically lasting. And a part of the narrative is: Getting into a high-paid professional is important; more so the idea that it has to be the right one.

Mine must be the universal experience of those brought by over-anxious parents. In one's teenage years, the dream of escape was passionate, romantic. The fit between petite bourgeois values and tiger parenting is tight. Yet, we all manage to find a way around it somehow. June Park, a Korean-American journalist, describes the educational choices she had faced:

> Early on, my parents wanted me to become a doctor, lawyer or engineer, and I had enrolled at UC Irvine as a biology major. But after a year and a half, and without consulting my parents, I got off the pre-med track and hopped a freight train heading nowhere: I chose to study not what was prestigious or respectable but what I loved (literature and philosophy). My parents stopped paying for my education, and I had to work as a temp and teaching assistant to put myself through the rest of college and graduate school. When I finally got my Ph.D., I asked my mother, "Are you proud of me now?" Her response was, "We never asked for that." This has not been good for our relationship.[6]

Yet she, in her own way, has reconciled with her parents.

> Sometimes you have to rebel, even if it means cutting yourself off from your parents. Obviously this isn't ideal – you end up with no family. I know from experience: I finally stood up to my mother two years ago and I haven't seen or spoken to any member of my family since. (Although I have exchanged e-mails with my father and siblings, and my mother and I are now "friends" on Facebook.)[7]

She has made the start; love and mutual understanding has turned her parents around. Park's handling of her parents is masterly and wise. She has found the balance between her parents' demands on her and her own self-esteem. She has a job that she finds fulfilling, not highly paid like medicine and law as her parents have wanted, but nonetheless a secure job that sustains her and her young family. You wish the same for Amy Chua's high-achiever children when they grow up. I have too easily dismissed tiger parenting for its audacity and boorish materialism. Its lasting effects have made me grave with misgivings. All the same, perhaps tiger parenting is not all unredeemed striving and professional success. And it seems to me the ultimate revenge is to imitate its anxiety, to harvest the energy of what is clearly an impossible idea. To work hard seven days a week on a job one finds fulfilling, with the modest financial security that goes with it, is to turn an adversary into a friend. In a sense I have owed a great deal to the orthodox Asian or Chinese childrearing. I had been toughed up, I got street-wise. And it was the tough-mindedness of a shophouse existence that had helped me to leave the parochialism and the 'culture is everything' insularity of Chinese petite capitalism. And it had propelled me to leave and make a home elsewhere in a foreign land.

## Notes

1. These include those funded by private capital, and foreign universities, mainly from the UK and Australia, which have set up offshore campuses—the so-called twinning programmes—in Malaysia.
2. Anthony Burgess, *The Malayan Trilogy*. NY: Random House, 2017.
3. Amy Chua, *Battle Hymn of the Tiger Mother*, NY: The Penguin Press, 2011.
4. For the politics of the Chinese education movement in Malaysia, see: Santhiram R. Raman and Yao Sua Tan. *The Development of Chinese Education in Malaysia: Problems and Challenges*. Singapore: ISEAS, 2015. Xia, Nan, Yanan Yang, and Yok Fee Lee. 'Chinese Education in Malaysia under Malaysian Ethnic Politics'. *J of Politics and Law* 11 (2), 2018, pp. 23–35.

5. Souchou Yao. "Books from Heaven: Literary Pleasure, Chinese Cultural Text and the 'Struggle Against Forgetting'". *The Australian Journal of Anthropology* 8 (3), 1997, p. 204.
6. Julie Park, 'On Tiger Mum'. https://thepointmag.com/2012/examined-life/on-tiger-moms. Accessed 6 June 2019.
7. Ibid.

## Bibliography

Barthes, Roland. 1979. *The Eiffel Tower and Other Mythologies*. Berkeley: University of California Press.

Burgess, Anthony. 2017. *The Malayan Trilogy*. NY: Random House.

Chua, Amy. 2011. *Battle Hymn of the Tiger Mother*, NY: The Penguin Press.

Santhiram R. Raman and Yao Sua Tan. 2015. *The Development of Chinese Education in Malaysia: Problems and Challenges*. Singapore: ISEAS.

Xia Nan, Yanan Yang and Yok Fee Lee. 2018. 'Chinese Education in Malaysia under Malaysian Ethnic Politics'. *J of Politics and Law* 11 (2): 23–35.

Yao, Souchou. 1997. 'Books from Heaven: Literary Pleasure, Chinese Cultural Text and the "Struggle Against Forgetting"'. *The Australian Journal of Anthropology* 8 (3): 190–209.

### Internet Resources

Julie Park, 'On Tiger Mum'. https://thepointmag.com/2012/examined-life/on-tiger-moms. Accessed 6 June 2019.

CHAPTER 7

# A Lesson on Borrowing

The feeling was one of helplessness. My father and I walked there three or four times a week to hand over the cash-like gifts to the god whose greed knew no bounds. Even the architecture was a cliché of avarice. From the road, you climbed up the stony steps and found yourself before a building with white Corinthian columns, at the door a couple of Malay guards cradling shotguns. Since its founding in 1932, the Overseas Chinese Banking Corporation (OCBC) had been, as they say, a Chinese community bank. In the 1970s, after the state reform had allowed Malay capital to buy into the bank, the OCBC had nonetheless kept its ethnic character, serving Chinese customers of all shades. Inside the bank we stood with other depositors before the cashier seated safely behind the metal grate. There were long queues all along the counters: men in threadbare golf shirts and frayed khaki trousers, women in plain polyester pants, all waiting to hand over their money. Between the temple of finance and its supplicants the divide was clearly drawn. None of us depositors were favoured with personal banking conducted inside the office, so we took our turn before the cashier. One by one the customers dropped off their money and stepped back to watch. Facing the riches, the cashier did not lift his eyes. He took a bundle and ran his pallid fingers over the cash. He made the count slowly, a pile at a time; his face soon given over to boredom. I watched with awe the proceedings. What my father and I had handed over was the arbiter of value, the reason why we had worked so hard at the High Street shop. If the bank was like a temple, I knew we worshippers would gain



S. Yao, *The Shop on High Street*,
https://doi.org/10.1007/978-981-15-2031-0_7

very little. It was a one-way traffic the money's journey to the bank. It seemed to my young mind colossally unjust. I mean, why couldn't some of the money come back our way? We could have used it to pay for the entertainment centre, or the Toyota sedan we coveted, or for the holiday in Thailand we had been talking about. As it was, we were mere conveyors of cash, conduits through which our sweat and earning would travel from the shop to their final destination.

Indebtedness was the fate of petite capitalists like my father. He was not a big operator, and his business turnover was too meagre for the bank to be interested in him. He was not a rubber trader or a tin merchant or building contractor, so he was not courted for his business. Redoubtable and solid on the hilltop, the bank suffered no embarrassment of riches. We needed the bank; the bank didn't need us. At the end, the cash we offered up could not atone for our insignificance.

Every small family business has a story to tell about its dire financial position. All the shopkeepers we knew said the same thing: cash was short, and the banks were greedy and tight-fisted, they would not serve us. As a result, the shopkeepers were sent begging to their friends and relatives. The route to financial solvency was tortuous, with many detours and dead-ends. Lucky for anthropology, this reliance on non-bank lenders was full of traditional notions and old-fashioned relationships that made up what is called the gift economy. The gift economy is strong on reciprocity and its ethics: goods and services given are returned in the name of the binding relationship between people. Instead of profit or personal gain, the gift economy emphasizes social continuity and community norms. David Graeber, author of the monumental *Debt: The First 5000 Years*, prefers the term human economy.[1] But he makes very much the same points. Debt and debt relationships are more than economic relationships; they have a social and political context; they define power relations between lenders and borrowers. *Debt* is work of grand historical sweep; it is polemical and politically engaged. The utopian vision has come out of Graeber's social activism—he was one of the leading figures of the 2011 Occupy Wall Street movement. His anti-capitalist stance is as a wet-nosed hound tracking and sniffing at an epic evil over 5000 years of human history. The work is rich in history, polished in analysis. Against the social and moral catastrophe of debt, Graeber turns to the human economy as a corrective to capitalism's excesses. Familiar to every anthropologist, the human economy is found in tribal societies and small urban communities. It relies on cooperation and reciprocity; it is personal and altruistic rather than competitive and self-regarding as in the modern capitalist society. Read with Graeber's polemics in mind, *Debt* patently makes a case for restoring the human economy and its powerful ethos back to the contemporary world.

It is hard to quarrel with a magnificent work like *Debt*. Its rhetorical elegance shames the less imaginative writers, and to say the devil in the details—in how to pit the argument against a real situation—is a lame criticism. But it is of enormous interest to me that the Chinese petite capitalists practise a form of exchange very close to Graeber's human economy. What takes place can be as Byzantine and complex as any age-old custom or ritual. Under Chinese petite capitalism, the human economy has become compressed, its ruling ethos intensified and articulated in different forms.

My father believed that financial dealings among friends must be honourable; there should be no 'more for me and less for you' self-interest and competition. His vision of the human economy shunned rivalry and tough bargaining; it is peaceful and considerate to both sides. The Chinese call this mode of transaction guanxi, the art of social connections. Guanxi incites the imagination of Chinese and foreign observers alike. The media talk about it, the business schools teach and celebrate it, the Chinese themselves are proud of it. As with the human economy, the guanxi economy too is concerned with upholding the social and moral order threatened by rampant self-interest.

Here the resemblance ends. If the human economy is political and anti-capitalist, the guanxi economy is conservative and avoids world-changing agendas. As one commemorates fairness and equitability, the other glosses materialist self-interests with the veneer of social harmony. My father was keen on the idea of the guanxi economy because it is the Chinese way of transaction, because it is full of moral and ethical affectations. Like when you are looking for a good buy at your uncle's used-car lot: you two are so close that a bit of hard bargaining would not cause ill in the relationship. Chinese business people are skilled dialecticians: they believe competition and altruism can be harmonized, their contradictions smoothed over.

We are rarely comfortable with debt. Debt is other people's money, and you go to the lender because you do not have money of your own to pay for what you need. But to incur debt implies a number of things: the poor state of your financial affairs, a certain recklessness that makes you live beyond your means, and you are less than a person for being indebted to others. Debt not repaid is a form of theft, and one can be brought before the courts to enforce repayment. The costs of debt are financial, social and moral.

For all the evils of debt Graeber exposes, it is also true that for most of us life is impossible without committing ourselves to some form of debt. None of us, except those with generous and wealthy parents, can buy a house or get a university education without borrowing. And businesses borrow to invest in tools and to upgrade the equipment, to hold stocks, to build factories and plants. For individuals and businesses alike, these are good debts that help them to accrue benefits or profits over a stretch of time.[2] However, individuals and businesses also borrow for the wrong reasons. Big corporations sometimes use borrowed fund to buy back shares in the stock market to jack up the company value; and people use credit cards and Cash Convertors to feed their 'buy now pay later' consuming habits. These are bad debts, debts people cannot afford and used for unproductive purposes. Good and bad, debt enables one to spend on things before one has the means to pay for them: the wonder of hire purchase. In any case, with debt purchasing decisions are no longer tied to the amount of money one actually has. There is a difference, of course. Good debt is liquidity, the stuff that greases the business machine; it helps one to buy a house before we have saved up for it. But bad debts are socially and morally damaging—Graeber's major grudge against debt.

Of the forms of debt, it is bad debt that concerns us. A loan borrowed and repaid on time or according to schedule causes little complications; it raises no issues of personal fault. But failing—or refusing—to repay one's debts is to default on one's obligation and responsibility, and deserves denunciation. Debt is more than a private affair between lender and borrower, but something that touches on broader social values and judgements.

In the spirit of his analysis, Graeber believes most debts are bad debts. Since debt affects a person's reputation, and imposes a troubled relationship between lender and borrower, an interesting departure is to examine social meaning of borrowing. In debt, money is exchanged for all kinds of things—obligation, power, fealty. In Britain, economic historians have turned to studying the social history of money and debt. One major work is Margot C. Finn's *The Character of Credit: Personal Debt in English Culture, 1740–1914.*[3]

The eighteenth century heralded the rise of modern capitalism. The ideas that stretch across the writings of John Locke to those of Adam Smith prepared the British economy for transition to free trade and the industrial revolution. The process brought about the transformation of British society and with that, the making of free individuals who thrived in an unfretted market economy. Finn's major task is to show that the social and economic transformation brought about by capitalism was neither total nor complete. In fact, the moral economy of the old society did not get left behind. The legacy of the past held its own, and continued to guide people's conduct and daily dealings.

Finn's central theme is debt and credit in British social life. One's credit or debt relationship said a lot about one's character—that loaded word in British society. In her reading of Samuel Johnson's *Pamela* and Henry Fielding's *Amelia*, Finn shows how the two heroines' sexual and moral personalities are caught up with the debts they have incurred. In *Pamela*, for the heroine to accept money or gifts, even without the expectation for repayment, ties her to her giver-donor who is also her patron and seducer. Eighteenth-century Britain had its own form of the gift economy. Both the giving and the receiving of gift or credit defined, in different ways, one's moral excellence or the lack of it. The villainous squire Mr B's manoeuvres are all about gift-giving and lending; he has tried to subdue Pamela's resistance by offering her his mother's clothes, and by advancing her parents money. Mr B's generosity is a kind of soft power based on class privilege. It tries to shame the recipients into acknowledging their lowly position, and it aims to pressure the heroine into submission. Money is a crude means of seduction, and the reader is gratified to find that she has seen through the deception and resisted.

In the novel, a clear line of moral worth is drawn between Mr B and Pamela his victim. Benevolence and virtue are bestowed upon a lender; gratitude, deference and a sense of obligations are extracted from a recipient. A debt relationship is an unequal relationship. As the lender gains in social esteem by saving the borrower from her financial woes, the borrower faces social disparagement of different shades. Pamela is scrutinized, her moral character is assessed. Speaking not only of Pamela, Finn writes: [In daily encounters,] 'creditors sought constantly and unsuccessfully to read debtors' personal worth and character from their clothing, their marital relations, their spending patterns and their perceived social status'[4]—a primitive but effective way of assessing a person's 'credit rating'.

An informant from a family of three generations of jewellers in Sydney once told me a Jewish aphorism: 'To sell a man pearls that you have got and that he wants, that is not business. To sell a man pearls that you have not got and that he does not want, that is business.' The miracle of business is salesmanship and the power of credit. Salesmanship breaks down the reluctant purchaser, making him buy something he does not want.

Selling what you don't have requires financing and incurring debt. This is the legendary 'making money with other people's money', which Chinese petite capitalists are besotted with. It is the height of all commercial wisdom. Getting a loan is to encroach on other people's resources. In accounting terms, credit is free money—if the profit can cover the interest, the cost of borrowing. It is easy to see the temptation and the greed. As an incentive to borrow, the principle is not unlike that of an investor who relies on marginal lending from the bank to finance his purchases, with the same pressure for the lender to recall the loan when it suits him. For the stock investor as for any petite capitalist, 'making money with other people's money' is adventurism, with a dash of devil-may-care heroism.

Chinese petite capitalists rely on social relationships. But the way of guanxi also imposes rules and judgements on borrowing and lending. The reality is: 'making money with other people's money' may be tempting, but it is financially and morally risky. The moral code about lending and debt can be as elaborate, as extravagant, as what was practised in eighteenth-century Britain. Among my father and his associates, lenders gained prestige and power, and debt affected the moral character of the borrower. The ethos of reciprocity was forceful and far reaching. Yet it is also the case that friends and associates and kin frequently lent to each other. They were all small businesspeople; they did not hold vastly different amount of wealth, and their relationship was reasonably equitable. There were no big players who only lent and did not borrow. At the same time, one's financial fortunes went up and down; a lender one day could become a borrower another day. This is quite a different situation that Graeber and Finn have described. In my father's world, if not in Graeber's, creditors and debtors are divided yet related in all kinds of ways. Here, no one was rich and dominant enough to impose his will on others. And in this world the creditor might decide to lend or not to lend, and he, too, was subject to the judgement of others. Like the borrower, the lender was gauged for his sincerity, his reputation, his financial position. The creditor-lender enjoyed no free ride in the relationship.

This explains a lot of my father's dealing with his major lender Iron Monger Lee. Their transaction, as I have described, was fraught with doubt on both sides. There was relief for both lender and borrower when the deal was done. There had not been a clear winner or a loser, or so it seemed. As power and dominance went to the lender's side, the borrower, in his own way, had also gained an upper hand. He had got Iron Monger Lee to lend without collateral. He had 'belittled' him with his big city ways, which sent Lee—ex-gangster and failed Chinese boxer—to cringing unworthiness. Lee had bragged and blustered, but I knew he was also somewhat in awe of my father and his prosperity and quiet dignity. Nonetheless, for all that divided them, they shared some common ideas about what kind of people they should deal with, about the background and social reputation of those with whom one should enter into a financial relationship. In a sense, they could not help but think of the bank: there, transactions are clear and modern, borrowing costs are lower and lending is secured. But both had stuck to the guanxi transaction; both were compromised. That afternoon in Sungei Buloh had revealed to me the insight: things can lean heavily *against* the lender, the dispenser of largess—not only against the likes of Pamela and her parents, the recipients of gifts and credit. Or better, both the lender and borrower are put through the grind of mistrust and financial overstretch and the oppressive feeling of obligation.

In my memory, the deposit-taking scheme is forever associated with the little yellow book issued to each person who put his or her money in the shop. Each page carried the headings: Date, Deposit, Withdrawal and Balance. On the cover was the chop of the High Street shop and the depositor's name. It was cheap stationary that belied the hope and optimism invested in it. Opened a page, you saw the array of figures running from top to bottom—evidence of one's saving habits and withdrawals and occasional reckless spending. With a deposit-taking system our position vis-à-vis the bank was reversed. We were taking in deposits; we were a recipient of other people's money. But we were a quasi-bank, not the real thing.

In Malaysian cities and small towns, there exists, as did in the past, an amorphous, highly diverse 'non-bank sector'. It consists of pawnshops, small shops like ours, Indian Chettier moneylenders, and for the really desperate, the Ah Long loan sharks.[5] These lenders, except the loan sharks, also take deposits. But lending is their main business, charging high interest rates calculated in weeks or months. These 'institutions' are popular among the poor, and their lending rates circulate in coffee shops and through the social grapevine. These are not banks, but they follow the same principles. High-risk lending attracts high interest charges; unsecured deposits enjoy high returns. As deposit-taker and borrower, the High Street shop did not escape these rules.

The non-bank money market—let's call it that—is neither free nor open. The loan sharks are desperate criminal types. For the borrowers, the cost of delayed repayment or default on a loan is high: an assault in a dark alley at night, a splash of red paint on the front door—a threat and a sign of shame. The pawnshops and moneylenders are less theatrical. Their approach is to personalize the customer relationship. Each pawnshop or moneylender tends to have its own set of clientele: the regulars who would go to the same lender when they need to borrow.

In Malaysia, the Indonesian maids are loyal customers of pawnshops which are practically all Chinese owned and operated. Accompanying Lastri on her visits, the anthropologist is impressed with her easy rapport and friendliness with the shop owner. They talk about news back home, she asks for the latest quote on gold and silver prices, and she pleads that the same discount be given in this round of transaction. The pawnbroker does his smooth talking: You are my special customer. Have I ever cheated you? There is goodwill on both sides, and the comforting assurance of a relationship built over time. We are before the counter, Mr Wong the pawnbroker is behind it. Outside a breath of breeze picks up and rattles softly the awning. It is a good day to do business. Lastri has just got paid—she works as a maid in a hotel resort—and has come to buy jewellery. It is not what it sounds like. She is not buying it for herself; she is buying it as a form of saving. She has been working for almost six years, and all her savings are tied up in gold jewellery which she keeps in the room that her hotel has provided. The earrings, the necklaces, the rings: they are secured and transferable—not holding cash is also an impediment against compulsive spending. When she needs money to send home, she would pawn a piece or two of the jewellery with Mr Wong, which she would later redeem on her payday.

Tagging along with Lastri, you are led into a world where banking takes on another name, where borrowing and lending is conducted through well-practised talk and social rituals, and the pawnshop is a homely institution that helps to meet one's financial needs. The transaction has been smooth and amicable.

Yet like true love, things don't always run smoothly. She panics when money is needed urgently at home—Lastri has been paying off in instalments a betor motorized-pedicab she bought for her husband. To secure a new loan calls for the right timing and the need to mortgage another piece of her jewellery. The well-greased system breaks down when there is a sudden spike in gold and silver prices against the ringgit, when her pay cheque is late and she lacks the cash to redeem a set of earrings or a bracelet used as a security. Frugal and wise, she plans ahead, and renegotiates with Mr Wong. Some of her friends are not so lucky; they never save enough to redeem their jewellery pieces. They face a cycle of repayments, and their debts accumulate.

Through their travails, it is not Lastri's and her friends' habit to go shopping for another pawnshop. Each has stayed with her pawnshop-lender. They have not gone on a search for another pawnshop, one perhaps more flexible with repayment schedules, one that might even pay better for their jewellery than the present lender. In actuality, such a lender does not exist. Gold and silver prices do not vary between the pawnshops—late quotes are delivered instantly on their mobile via text or WhatsApp. There are discounts for regular customers, but they are so minor as to be negligible. So Lastri and her friends stay loyal to their lenders. But for them loyalty is a word of many shades of meaning. They have in mind the discounts and the most favourable prices. But they also want to conduct their financial affairs in a congenial environment, where trust and a good personal relationship are important. It is better to stay in a proven relationship than to jump ship at the first sign of difficulties. This is not textbook economic rationality, but it does signal that the lender and the borrower exist in the same cultural universe, where people are assured of their relationships and their transactions do not go awry.

Even in my father's days in the seventies, the pawnshops and Chettier moneylenders and Ah Long loan sharks served customers across the ethnic communities. Penury equalizes: the Chinese, the Indians and the Malays shared the same pick of non-bank credit providers. (At the school gate the end of each month, I remember, the Chettier moneylender put a small desk before which our teachers lined up to pay their debts—then he went on to the Methodist Boys' School and its teachers next door.) The Chinese deposit takers were shops like ours; they were 'banks' that accepted deposits not to lend but only for their own use. As a rule, each recruits the depositors from its community. It was the Cantonese putting their money in Cantonese shops, the Fukienese putting their cash in Fukienese shops and so on. The High Street Shop's depositors were practically all Hakka kinfolks. Our dealings with them were amiable, and kind of cosy. The social nature of lending and borrowing means exactly that. Since the depositors were our kinfolk, we appealed to our customary relationship. We would not cheat them; it's safe for them to leave their money with us. We would not, like the bank, wheedle them with fancy logos and awe-inspiring building and shotgun cradling guards, but they could rely on our reputation and the fact that we were related. We did not treat them like bank customers and we gave out no illusions of power and grandeur.

As a borrower, what did we want from the setup? Well, we wanted, as would any deposit-taking institution, stability and liquidity. Stability suggested a viable system over time—that the flow of deposits and withdrawals was orderly and sustainable. The system should run smoothly and peacefully, like the proverbial brook in the English countryside. There should be no sudden spikes in transactions. Big deposits created a rush of riches we did not need and could not afford to pay back; but this rarely happened. Liquidity ensured that a level of cash was available for the depositors when they needed it. A bank run—the failure to meet customers' withdrawals—would be a disaster. Remember Frank Capra's *It's a Wonderful Life*? For George Bailey as for my father, formally such a disaster can be averted by the goodwill of the community from which the depositors have been recruited. A lot of pain and trouble is embroiled in the easy principle: we needed the depositors to leave their money in the shop, and we wanted them not to make large withdrawals without giving us notice.

Thus both borrower and depositors demanded from each other consistency—erratic behaviour is not good for anyone. Both must be, in different ways, honourable and trustworthy; the borrower-lender relationship must enjoy a degree of certainty in order to keep afloat the financial system.

We called her Auntie Mei, an expression of respect and the fact we were kin. She was in her early forties, and her slow way of speaking gave the impression she was meek and long suffering. But she could be a chatter box when she wanted to. And because she was comfortable with my parents, during her visit she would open up about her children, her backache and rheumatism, her night market stall and her disparagement of her husband—'A stupid man!'—that hinted at domestic discord. My parents didn't want to pry, but she was doing all the talking and my parents smiled and listened. With her deposits, she preferred to leave the details with my father, not questioning the balance or the returns. She was, in short, a perfect customer. And when she made a call for withdrawal, it was 100 or 200 ringgit, never more.

One day, when she began to ask to make for more withdrawals, often two or three times a month, our antenna—our self-interest—was raised. We couldn't refuse, of course. My father would ask her each time he handed her the money: Is there some trouble at home? Or he would say: It is not good to take out so much, it is your hard-earned money—unless you really need it. And she would turn on a quizzical look as she pocketed the money, mumbled a few words and left. Her demeanour had changed, we noticed. She was quiet and she was no more the loquacious woman who complained about her husband and her rheumatism.

A couple of weeks later, a craggy-faced man came by the shop and asked for my father. He was Auntie Mei's brother, he said. His sister had got into putting money in the back-lane betting shop. It was 10 ringgit here and 20 ringgit there, but she couldn't afford it, he said. He lived next door to her sister, and knew the situation. He then asked my father: Can you do something (to stop her from spending her savings)? My father promised he would do what he could, reminding him that the money was hers and she was free to spend it as she liked.

During her next visit an awkward hospitality was forced upon her. My parents guided her to the kitchen and brought up the subject. Her response was: Did my brother come to see you? He shouldn't have, he shouldn't come and bother you. She tried to make light of what her brother had revealed. It was a couple of ringgit now and then, she said, just to pass the time. She listened to my father and did not take offence. In any case, perhaps she wasn't yet an addict, just thrilled at the occasional wins, Auntie Mei was talked out of her betting habits and returned to her regular regime of small, manageable withdrawals.

Auntie Mei continued to keep an account with us. We congratulated ourselves. We were kin, nonetheless we felt we had meddled in her domestic affair. But no damage was done, and we were relieved. My parents' intervention had paid off.

The end of her gambling habit put a stop to the bleeding of her account. Over the months she put in deposits when she could, her balance eventually reaching near 15,000 ringgit. It was a large sum for someone like her—and a burden for us when she was to ask for it.

Auntie Mei's second son was a bright-eyed eighteen-year-old, who just finished high school at the top of his class. He had risen from the village school, with its poor teachers and rowdy classes, and earned a place in a school in the nearby town half-an-hour's bicycle ride away from home. After graduation, he added to his achievements by winning a Taiwanese government scholarship to study aquaculture at a university in Kaohsiung city. One Saturday morning, his mother brought him to meet us, and to receive my parents' blessing. The boy was tall, lanky and smart looking. I remember thinking: Auntie Mei is right not to get him a job in a shop and become one of the army of shopboys, for he is made for better things. She brushed aside our praise, but her voice was full of pride. Then she came to the point: she wanted to ask to take out the whole of the 15,000 ringgit.

She would use some of the money to fix up the roof of her house, the rest would go towards getting his son fitted out for the journey and to help him to settle in when he arrived. The hosts and their guests continued with their soft shuffling of words. Mother and son had stayed on, and we drank and talked until it was decent for them to leave.

In the following days my father did a number of things. He shifted money from some other accounts to make ready for Auntie Mei when she would come for her money. He staggered the invoices; those who needed immediate payments were catered for; others were renegotiated over the phone. Mostly the exercise was to cream off amounts from the richer accounts. And we sought out the duplicitous but seemingly reliable Iron Monger Lee. We once again endured the lukewarm Oolong tea and the Bruce Lee demonstration; but he somehow came good, much to our relief.

The way we had dealt with Auntie Mei confirmed to a set of principles. An account holder would be talked out of making a large withdrawal as courtesy permitted, when financial good sense dictated that the depositor would not do so. But we were pressed by social considerations. How could we ask Auntie Mei to leave her money when she had good reasons to demand it this time? And there was no better, no more legitimate reason than sending a son or a daughter to the university—or a wedding in the family, or setting up a small business. For us, the decision was: how much of a depletion of our balance we should allow. We had to gauge the bad feelings we would cause when we tried oppose any withdrawal. We had to trade off the sentiment of kinship against our own interest.

And then there was the shuffling of the account balances. It was financial management on a knife's edge. It worked by servicing one account through drawing on another account. And it stalled the risk of insolvency by poaching the resources of one or more account holders. The result was to spread the risk like contagion over the whole system.

There is a banking lore that says: A large borrower puts a bank at his mercy, a small borrower puts himself at the bank's mercy. The logic is simple. A larger borrower is a big debtor; he owes the bank a substantial amount. Together with other debtors, his default threatens to undo the bank and holds it to ransom. On the other hand, a bank can afford to ignore the small debtors—and often do by writing off their loans. Their default causes but a small dent on the bank's substantial holding. Thus the point: a large debtor enjoys a certain power vis-à-vis the bank in a way a small debtor does not. This is clearly discernible in the situation facing the High Street shop: the more seriously the shop came to depend on a set of depositors, the greater the threat they posed. For the deposits never lay idle. They had been slotted into many uses in making the business solvent. The devil was the ever-pressing need for liquidity. The demand for cash was like so many puppies sucking on a bitch's tits, hungry and insatiable. It made the never-ending cycle of deposit taking and putting the deposits to use an undertaking of enormous dexterity, which brings to mind the infamous Ponzi investment scheme.

For all its manoeuvring and moral duplicity, the Ponzi investment scheme is not difficult to understand. It takes the idea of 'making money with other people's money' to its logical height. Investors are attracted by the high returns, much higher than what conventional institutions would offer, forgetting that too good to be true is exactly that. Soon the returns would cease coming, when the payments to the investors prove unsustainable. For there has not really been a reserve, a fund put aside to meet withdrawals and the distribution of returns. The solution right from the beginning has been to recompense one set of investors by shifting money from another set of investors. The scheme is heavily leveraged. Debts are built upon on debts, and the pressure is high in bringing in fresh investors, a fresh stream of victims greedy and gullible. The suitable metaphor is a mouse in a wheel, nervous and unstoppable. Everything about the Ponzi scheme is loud, it is morally vacuous and damaging to people's lives.

This is not quite how the deposit-taking system worked at the High Street shop. There were no crooked financial advisors, there were no PR men and women pushing glossy pamphlets to senior citizens. Yet the narrative has inexorably taken us here.

The Ponzi-like practices at the High Street shop were due to the wilful neglect by banks. They were acts of desperation; and they had much to do with the customary ways of the small Chinese family business. What happened was not quite honourable, but if an excuse be needed we had been forced into it. In any event, it brought about a financial disaster and we were punished for it. But what of the depositors? With a scheme so full of risk, so dependent on the moral character of the 'banker', what did the depositors get out of it? We had not tried to ensnare anyone, but we did offer an eight per cent return for their investments, more or less twice the fixed deposit rates of the banks. The high returns were a major incentive. But the problem for us was the depositors' poor tolerance for the system's occasional bottleneck, when the withdrawal was slow in coming through, when the boss was making excuses why it was so. When that happened, my father's assuring words sounded uneasy even to the most loyal depositors.

But none took these as cause for suspicion. If they had trusted the 'banker', they had trusted too much to the point of being blind to the reality that had been created.

It is bad social science to speak of economic rationality and quick seizing of opportunities for personal gain. Every decision made, every situation to which one has committed has moments of stasis. Lodged in a web of social relationships, the depositors were committed to a deposit scheme they had found appealing and stayed with it. The reasoning may be too breezily casual, but it propelled the decision nonetheless. Like the Indonesian women and their pawnshops, the depositors wanted a 'banker' who is known to them, with whom they shared an easy rapport. They recognized how Chinese small shops operated. The High Street shop had delivered a good return, and it had provided order and certainty to financial matters often too complex for them. In a world full of crooks out to cheat the average folks, the trust they enjoyed with the boss did not feel blind or unreasonable.

Uncertainty rules every aspect of our life, except death—and the need to pay tax, as the cynic would say. Uncertainty is a major concern of businesses, the other is risk. Uncertainty makes planning and projection near impossible. Risk on the other hand points to contingencies and defaults of various sorts, and allowances are made for what these may bring. Businesses worry about tax, but their response tends to be: 'We don't mind paying tax but we need to know how much.' The response is cavalier, but pointing out that tax is unavoidable and the better wisdom is to make provisions for it. Businesses crave profit, but profit-taking needs certainty and the management of risk. In *Keynes: The Return of the Master*, the economic historian Robert Skidelsky revisits the issue. Uncertainty, he points out, is at the centre of Keynes' thinking.

> The centrepiece of Keynes's theory is the existence of inescapable uncertainty about the future, [a thinking that came out of] his experience as an investor during the turbulent period of the Great Depression. Taking uncertainty seriously – which few economists today do – has profound implications not just for how one does economics and how one applies it, but for one's understanding of practically all aspects of human activity. It helps explain the rules and conventions by which people live.[6]

Keynes had pushed for massive government intervention to even out the 'bust and crisis' cycle of the capitalist economy. However, Keynes also believed public spending should be discharged in an environment of reasonable certainty. It should not be left to the self-adjusting profit-seeking market because it is full of risk and uncertainty, because it is a poor decider of public investment's return and efficiency. Economists are concerned with risk and uncertainty in their understanding of how businesses work, but Keynes believed uncertainty, not risk, is the issue of greater concern. Skidelsky clarifies:

> Risk refers to situations in which we have good statistical data so that we can talk meaningfully about the probability that a particular event will happen, like the probability of a 70-year-old man dying within the next year. Uncertainty refers to situations in which we have no statistical basis to go on.[7]

Uncertainty is exactly that; it cannot be predicted, a mystery and an unknown with no basis for prediction. Risk can be managed or averted, and it has the virtue of being measurable and thus knowable. The world's economies, Skidelsky reminds us, are largely governed by structural conditions that cannot be measured, whose effects cannot be forecast.

There is a serious problem in the single-minded focus on risk: it tends to distort—and belittle—what defines most people's daily decisions. 'Keynes would have been utterly opposed to financial innovation beyond the bounds of ordinary understanding, and therefore control', Skidelsky writes.[8] Thinking of Lastri and her friends, it is clear what concerns them is the fickleness of human commitment, the uncertainty of the worth of things in which they have invested their money. They speak of bayaha—risk, danger, the hazards of life. But they mean uncertainty and the desire to put it under control.

Uncertainty also concerned our depositors. I don't believe even the most naïve among them would think their investment—or life—was without risk. But risk was perceived in different shades of vagueness. Life is full of bad luck, and people can't always be trusted, they said. All the same, they did not believe the boss would run away with their money, and the shop would go under—extraordinary events not likely to happen everyday. Risk is like fate, they had accepted it and they believed it could be 'managed' by being cautious and by picking the right shop that was solid and whose boss had a good reputation. Still, there was large measure of things that could not be foreseen, that no amount of attention and vigilance could hamper. This was uncertainty: the dire side of risk or danger.

Personal trust is at best mutual; it binds two people in a relationship where words and promises mean something. There is trust, and there is blind trust, which, like blind faith, is absolute and fundamental. What prevailed among the High Street shop and its depositors was not blind trust but a trust with a good deal of realism. My father's relationship with Auntie Mei—and even that with the rustic Iron Monger Lee—had a history. Each set of relationship had come out of a series of social dealings that confirmed the character and the trustworthiness of both partners. There was a lot of to and fro, a lot of testing each other's deeds and intentions. Against the regards and sentiments, each had to prove to the other that he or she was neither a bluffer nor a cheat. People were never too trusting, or too cynical as to put under suspicion everything others had said and done. There was mawkishness on both sides, but their trust in each other was not witless or total.

Yet it was this kind of half-trust that had created a degree of stability in the deposit-taking scheme. It was trust that allowed my father to intervene in Auntie Mei's affair without causing too much embarrassment for either. Uncomfortable things were said, but the relationship was not endangered. Once committed to leave the money in the shop, Auntie Mei's behaviour was levelled out. She trusted but not too much, she resisted my father's pressure not to make withdrawals but she also knew when to give over to his advice. She weighed, she assessed, she checked her own impulses. On my father's part, the trick was, as always, being judicious with what you said, and how to say it. A ground of certainty was created by the thoughtfulness and consideration—from both sides. The deposit system's stability was heavily hedged by all this; but it was stability nonetheless.

The deposit-taking system worked right until my father died. It was creative, a demonstration of the ingenuity of a desperate man. It had kept the family business afloat, and it had financed the wholesale venture my father had just started. But there had also been enormous pressure on our daily life. What are the key lessons of the deposit system? As a form of borrowing, you have to recruit depositors who trust you and your business. And there were enormous apprehensions about many things: the pressure of withdrawals, the moral compromises of being a debtor, the awful sense of being obligated to the kinfolks who lent us money. As a child I didn't have the juvenile fantasy of running away from home, but I had the vague wish for the fake-banking setup to fail. This is a story of the borrower-deposit taker and his family. Culture and social dealings explained the stability of the scheme. But even the child in me felt the stability to be a half-way measure. The anxiety was not allayed. Neither the shop nor our temperament allowed too much wishful thinking. Trust had provided the financial scheme's stability, but it was also its source of structural weakness. With both depositors and the shopkeeper, the nagging question was: in the course of endless social transactions, how would you know if you were too trusting, or if you were not trusting enough? It was a delicate balance not easy to achieve. And for most of the depositors the tendency was to opt for over-trusting.

The trouble with this kind of trust is that it was personalized; it was attached to a person. Unlike the OCBC building, the High Street shop itself did not generate awe and power. People did not trust the shop for its building, not really, but for the shopkeeper and his reputation. Personalism planted in the depositor's mind the idea: things can go wrong, but trust the boss, he'll take care of problems when they happen. It was always the boss himself, and the moral character which he wore like armour. When they trusted too much, they turned trust into faith which is always to a degree blind. And remember: the Ponzi system works not only because of the investors' greed and gullibility, but also because of their blind faith in the scheme and in those who run it. My father had held up the deposit-taking scheme on his shoulder, and the scheme collapsed dramatically when he died. At the creditors' meeting, I remember, there were two groups of men and women. There were those who had only half-trusted: they believed life as much mortals like my father were less than absolutely trustworthy. They were less affected because they had also invested their money elsewhere; they had not put all their eggs in one basket. Then there were those who had trusted my father and the scheme absolutely. In return they had enjoyed the sense of security the more cautious had not. The need for certainty had cost them. These depositors felt betrayed. They were scorned by a man they had held in too high a regard. For the Ponzi scheme as much as our deposit-taking setup, the idea of the proverbial free lunch rings true; their high returns are neither free nor morally unencumbered.

## Notes

1. David Graeber, *Debt: The First 5000 Years*. New York: Melville House, 2014.
2. It may be argued that student debts are 'good debts', given the view that education is a right for tax-paying citizens and a form of social investment that benefits the society, and should be forgiven.

3. Margot C. Finn, *The Character of Credit.* Cambridge: Cambridge University Press, 2003.
4. Ibid., p. 21.
5. See 'Loan sharks sharpen their bite'. https://www.thestar.com.my/news/nation/2018/01/20/loan-sharks-sharpen-their-bite-attractive-packages-for-major-events-aim-to-lure-more-victims/. Accessed June 27, 2018.
6. Robert Skidelsky, *Keynes: Lesson of the Master.* New York: Public Affairs, 2009, p. xv.
7. Ibid, pp. xiii.
8. Ibid, p. xvi.

## Bibliography

Graeber, David. 2014. *Debt: The First 5000 Years.* NY: Melville House.

Finn, Margot C. 2003. *The Character of Credit.* Cambridge: Cambridge University Press.

Skidelsky, Robert. 2009. *Keynes: Lesson of the Master.* NY: Public Affairs.

### Internet Resources

'Loan sharks sharpen their bite'. https://www.thestar.com.my/news/nation/2018/01/20/loan-sharks-sharpen-their-bite-attractive-packages-for-major-events-aim-to-lure-more-victims/. Accessed June 27, 2018.

CHAPTER 8

# Wholesale: The Road to Ruin

I went away filled with memories of my tropical childhood; four years later, I finished university and returned to face the closure of the High Street shop. Much had happened to me in those four years in Australia. My father had been sick and passed away, and the High Street shop, leaderless, limped on and waited for its end. During my time away I earned an Economics degree; my life experience was bolstered by working in a Chinese takeaway and by the hours spent reading in magnificent Barr Smith Library at the university. The student's life had not been for me one of ivory-tower complacency. I was young and gaining confident. You grow up quickly when you have to face ordeals you are not prepared for. Once again at home I told my mother I would look after things from now on. My elder brother and his family had moved to Perth, Australia, and it was left to me to take the helm and see the shop through its last days.

I am lucky to have lived in a small Chinese family business and witnessed its heydays and its end. Chinese petite capitalism is a world of hard work, perseverance and promiscuous optimism. At times, it feels like a hangover from the past—with its reliance on kinship, personal qualities and what anthropologists call the human economy, for its dealings. My father went through the rigmarole of these methods. When difficulties arose, he believed that the kindness of friends and kin, as much as his social reputation, would afford a solution. And he was mostly right. But he died before he could face the calamity that was unleashed on the family business and those burdened with its legacy.



S. Yao, *The Shop on High Street*,
https://doi.org/10.1007/978-981-15-2031-0_8

The story of the shop's insolvency began with my father's decision to expand into wholesale.

My father's aim was to increase the shop's earnings, but he was also forced into it. His values were middle ground; he was pragmatic and quick to make compromises in a situation of conflict. He was not a man who took too many risks. Yet, like most petite capitalists, he kept a keen eye for new opportunities. Cautious and conservative, he could also be spirited and innovative. He could not ignore the fact that wholesale was quite simply the next rung of accomplishment a modest shopkeeper could hope to reach.

When my father wrote to me about his plan, my thought was: he was playing down the risks, he did not talk about how to raise capital to finance the new venture. Later he wrote that the capital would mainly come from the depositors who had invested their savings in our shop, and he would recruit more depositors by hiking up the interest rates. I didn't say much, but I knew he would be committing himself to a level of debt he could not afford. I had just read Schumpeter's *Capitalism, Socialism, and Democracy*, and was struck by the sense of the tragic and human volatility the author imparts to his vision of economic progress.[1] In my mind I half-worried for my father, yet thrilled by his boldness and imagination. Isn't this what Schumpeter meant when he wrote that an entrepreneurial undertaking is a mixture of invention, economic foresight and bold leadership?[2]

My father's plan gradually came to fruition. He wrote to me about his visits to this 'uncle' and that 'auntie' to raise money, the hectic pace of work at the shop. He told me he had taken on a few more shopboys, and how busy he and the whole family were. I remember arriving home one day during the university vacation. I stepped into the shop from the taxi, and found myself in a busy scene: the workers queuing before the lorry to unload; the shop floor littered with bundles of goods waiting to be packed and sent away, while normal trade went on at the sales counter. I rushed upstairs with my luggage, changed my clothes and came down to help. I couldn't load and unload the lorry, but I could pack the goods in carton boxes and mark on each the name and address of the shop it was to go to. Some would be sent by lorries, but most would be squeezed into the van and delivered directly to the customers. My father was speaking over the phone, my mother overseeing what was going on with keen eyes and my sister serving lunch in the kitchen where workers took turn to eat. There was an infectious sense of collective labour and I was making myself a part of it. Wholesale was taking the shop—and our lives—to a new direction. My misgivings were swept away.

In the front seats of the Volkswagen Kombi, the ride was smooth with occasional bumps to jolt us out of the grogginess of a long journey. Yoke Lim, one of the senior counter-men, was at the wheel. We had started out at six-thirty to avoid the morning traffic. We had driven thorough the city, and now the road turned into a convoy of lorries and van and buses and passenger cars. We went past a strand of factories and small settlements at the city's fringe. The road was now flanked by long stretches of green: the neat rubber plantations, the oil palms and, beyond in the far hills, the dense jungle that seemed to follow us as we made our way further into the rural hinterland.

Rural hinterland—or villages—was a bit of a misnomer, actually. During the Malayan Emergency (1947–60)—the British and later the Malaysian government's effort to cull a communist uprising—the authorities had put almost a million people into resettlement centres. They were called new villages, to give them a sense of the rural idyll. From within the barbed wire fences, people left each morning through the checkpoints to work in the rubber plantations and tin mines and farms; and in the new villages people opened shops, children went to school and young mothers took their babies to the health clinics set up as part of winning 'hearts and minds' of the rural folks.[3] A trip to the new villages never failed to thrill me with their association with communist insurrection and British counterinsurgency. After the defeat of the communists, the new villages had grown and morphed into small townships, each with its working population and a vibrant economy. And businesses spilled from small towns to what remained of the new villages and to the shops at the rural fringes. These shops were remote; they lay outside the main roads and were isolated. The big wholesalers were not interested in them; but for shopkeepers like my father, these rural shops were an opportunity. A wholesale business set up to supply them would require small capital and relatively simple operation—using a van and the driver-salesman to take orders and make deliveries.

We had left the highways a while ago; the asphalt road narrowed, then dipped. We slowed down, and the car was holding on to a dirty road—a trail of dust rising behind us. Before us, the view was marked by clusters of grass huts—each with attap roof and mud walls, looking picturesque but a bit desolate against the jungle's green expanse. The shops were outside the new villages proper, and scattered. It took us about half an hour or so to cover the distance from shop to shop. These shops, and the rustic men and women who ran them, were our customers. When we stopped, they came out to greet us. They were reserved and dusty folks, but happy to see us. We had filled their orders and brought them the goods, and we had carried news from the city; so perhaps they were genuine in their welcome.

Hong Fatt Store—'Bright and Prosperous Store', Chinese petite capitalists gave their stores auspicious names—was our first stop. The owner Ah Lau and his wife greeted us at the shopfront. They were in their sixties; their bodies stooped slightly when they walked; they had coarse hands and sun-stained faces. They made me, the boss' son, sit down under the awning and thrust a warm Pepsi in my hand. Mrs Lau asked about my parents; I told her they are well and they sent their best wishes. It was vacuous chit-chat that stood for good manners. I made an excuse and went out to help Yoke Lim to sort out the goods in the van. We dug through the pile and found what we were looking for. It was a small order—the invoice was about 350 ringgit, but we treated it as if grand purchase of a big shop owner. We carried the few cartons out, and piled them neatly on the shopfloor. Seeing his order, Ah Lau perked up and began to go through the items one by one against the invoice. Tiger Balm and Eagle Medicated Oil and the like warranted no scrutiny. As he opened the packs of herbs and ran his hands over the dong gui roots and ginkgo berries, he muttered: 'They are such poor quality, not like the old days; and their prices are going up all the time!' He said it less for our ears than for his need to grumble and whine. I thought to myself: 'Well, they are low grade stuff because that's all you can afford.' He lifted himself from the floor, and as he stood up, he leaned against the counter to steady himself. The quick ascent from the ground made him dizzy, like a person with low blood pressure. He looked worn out. Life at the jungle fringe made him look grim, like a social outcast. I was ready with my sympathy, but the business of buying and selling made me hold back.

The place had no name. It was simply called Third Mile, after the distance from the nearest town. It was a small settlement of huts and stores of corrugated tin roofs and low brick walls. Beyond Hong Fatt Store were more stores and huts, grimy spots on the roadside that made you think of lorry stops no longer in use. But these were our customers; they were tired and jaded and they were not showy. And I reminded myself they worked hard like we did at the High Street shop. My father would have certainly identified with them, and he had picked his customers spreading over an area which the van and its driver could comfortably cover in a day. He had been like a cartographer mapping out the intricate pathways of a newly discovered territory. Each time the driver and I made the journey, it felt everything had been thought out, each destination carefully marked. We searched out for the retailer, made the delivery, received payments for the last invoice, took fresh orders and moved on to the next. The stores had signs written in Malay on top of the Chinese ones, as the official regulations required. The first stop was at Hong Fatt Kedai Runcit or Hong Fatt Provision Store, the nearest detour from the highway, which then continued on, to Sam Lim Kedai Runcit, and further, to Wan Chan Kedai Ubat or Wan Chan Medicine Shop. Each was modest and unremarkable; each was run by a husband-and-wife team whose efforts were like a valiant stand against the isolation and hopelessness of their shop by the jungle.

With the wholesale business, my father had again spoken of helping out the Hakka kinfolk. Kinship was a part of it, but competition and relative advantage also drove him. The High Street shop was a late comer, and the retail businesses in the new villages and townships had all but been carved up by the large city operators who fed the voracious consumer needs of the countryside: from car tyres to portable electric generators, from food to medicine, from clothing to footwear. What remained untapped was the settlements beyond: the small traders at the jungle fringes that so easily called up a sense of Conradian gloom. It was these traders who were the target of my father's wholesale venture.

He had not taken the decision lightly. He was sensible to the economic potential of the market, and the financial resources needed to get the scheme up and running. He knew he would have to raise more funds, and that meant, once again, turning to our friends and relatives. As for the customers, he would have to give the retailers the customary thirty-day credit. And he would have to wrestle profit from the purchases these traders could afford—by offering cheap, poor grade herbs; by promoting merchandise of less known brands; by brow-beating them with salesmanship when he could get away with it. All of this required careful budgeting, and the balancing of trust and risk in the customer relationship—as always, the human side of business.

For the time being, the problem was how to get the goods to the retailers. We had used the lorries of transport companies, but they were expensive. The alternative was the buses that plied the country roads. Before passing a shop, the driver would slow down and let the conductor toss off the merchandise onto the front of the premises. It was clumsy; goods often did not survive the rough handling. We realized the best way was to have our own vehicle to directly reach the customers. With our own van or small lorry, goods would be delivered safely, and there would be the additional advantage of keeping personal contacts with the retailers. And my father was half-thinking of social appearance: we needed a new vehicle to inaugurate the bold venture. In my memory, the wholesale business is forever associated with the super-modern, reliable VW Kombi van. At the VW dealership, the wonders of German engineering had got into my father. It was spacious and fuel-efficient, it was air-cooled—it had no radiator: the sales talk was infectious and irresistible. My father was sold and signed the purchase agreement. The VW Kombi was a symbol of hope, like a ship sail off the harbour, untroubled by the choppy sea at the horizon.

My father had spoken of the opportunities to be found at the rural fringes. But it is also true that the High Street shop had reached its structural limits, and wholesale was his way out. Petite capitalist enterprise is cursed by 'shortages' in many aspects. The capital and the yearly turnovers are small, the workers are transient and eager to move on to better jobs, and the operating costs are small and so are the earnings. The operation is squeezed on so many fronts. My parents didn't draw a wage, neither did the elder children who helped in the shop—though food and electricity bills were taken care of by the business expenses. The shopboys were paid a token wage; their labour was almost free. On the other hand, the shop kept long trading hours; the idea was to catch the customers when most shops were closed. The bulk of the daily sales consisted of popular items like Panadol and Tiger Balm, Scott's Cod Liver Emulsion and Marmite, as well as the herbal medicines prescribed by the doctor. These were items with small profit margins. But their turnover was quick; they did not stay long on the shelf and tie up capital. ('Dead inventory is dead money') The insight did not escape my father: the return from the popular merchandise and patent medicine was meagre, but if the sales were quick and in large volumes, the ceiling of annual return would be lifted. Profit would improve, and the business' structural limit would be broached.

For my father this must have been the Schumpeter moment. Innovation and far-sightedness were needed to get himself out of the financial dead end. Wholesale was the solution, and it would set him apart from other small shopkeepers. Perhaps this had been in his mind all the time: hard work and its virtue are all very well, but with wholesale he would be joining the league of big operators, wealthy merchants of face and social renown.

Wholesale involves a fairly straightforward principle. What entails invites the clear eye of an accountant. The wholesaler buys in large quantities directly from the manufacturers or the distributers, and resells them to retailers. The wholesaler straddles between the manufacturers of goods and the retailers who sell to the consumers. The position gives the wholesaler a strong advantage. Wholesale enables him to buy in bulk and receive a discount, and he earns a margin of profit when he resells to the retailers. From manufacturer to wholesaler to retailer, each makes a cut through the chain until it reaches the consumers. The wholesaler is invisible to the final consumers, but he ensures the flow of goods from factories to retailers, and the more rapid the flow, the more efficient the extraction of profit by each player. In the eyes of small retailers, the wholesaler enjoys a certain grandeur: he keeps a warehouse and holds large stocks; he has put a big investment into the business. In my father's time, the most prosperous retailers of Chinese medicine were also wholesalers.

That, in any case, was the general principle.

The greatest challenge facing every wholesaler is the need for capital. Capital is needed to make large purchases, and for meeting the costs of storage in keeping a warehouse. And capital is needed to meet the dead zone between sales made and the payment by the retailers. After goods have been sent and the invoice has been issued, thirty-day credit spells bottleneck and uncertainty. When wholesale is financed by the bank, there will be additional pressure from the lender. Wholesale is heavily leveraged. Loan facilities grease the system, and the pressure from the lender flows down the chain to the retailers who are squeezed to fulfil their debt obligations. This is the troubling side of wholesale.

I may recall with nostalgia the joyful family labour; I may wax lyrical about the journey to the rural stores in their breath-taking jungle setting; in truth, our wholesale business eventually turned out to be a catastrophe. It was exciting and promising, but it had also brought a good deal of financial stress and unhappiness. My father was not one to show his worries in front of the children. Nonetheless I recall in those days when his letters were full of money issues: how he needed to raise funds for the big order he had just made, or how he would badger the relatives to put in larger deposits than they normally would. When I was home, I used to listen to the conversations of my parents in the sitting room. The ripple of voices travelled to my room, full of urgency. I recall too kinfolk like Auntie Mei whose call for large withdrawals had caused panic. The deposit-taking scheme I previously described had been set up mainly to finance the wholesale business. And wholesale was the reason for my father to resort to the Ponzi-like juggling of accounts that led to the shop's bankruptcy.

Right until she passed away more than a decade after her husband, my mother thought the wholesale business had been a mistake, a curse. It was reckless; it had got the High Street shop heavily into debt. She was adamant about her assessment: it was the debts that had caused the shop's demise and our father's early death. She was bitter, and inconsolable about the shop's miserable end. Everything about the last days of the High Street shop—the shame, the bankruptcy, the string of people we owed money to, the relatives in the countryside left in the lurch following the bankruptcy—was due to the wholesale business. Was she right?

My mother, wise in her quiet and submissive way, had seen it coming. She had lived with her husband's busily scheming and petite capitalist dream. If he was sometimes blinded by his ambition, my mother was grounded. Keeping her eyes on the shop, she was cursed with knowing what was going on but helpless to do much about it. The hectic daily goings-on, the tension in the shop floor, the shortfall at the till on a bad day—they had depressed her. The tiff between my parents was not easily hidden. She raised the issues of what she had witnessed; she tried to get her husband to slow down the borrowing and spending. But her protest got nowhere, so it seemed.

My father had a temperament neither conservative nor reckless. Even a petite capitalist can be a bundle of contradictions. Stable and risk-averse, my father also had a restless mind. He liked the ancient classics and recordings of the Peking opera, but he also took to the writings of Lu Xun and Ba Jing for their modern, progressive thoughts. We believed the adults to be dinosaurs, but I remember how he had given in to the salesman's eager endorsement of the VW Kombi van—all German engineering and air-cooled engine—at the showroom. At home we had flipped through the glossy pamphlet: even he could not resist the modern design and super comfort and removable seats. Another quotidian note: my father was fond of the Westerns, especially those featuring John Wayne. We went to see *The Searchers* in the Rex Cinema in the Chinatown area. He enjoyed the great expanse of the American landscape, and he found the horse chase and the fistfights exciting. And he would ask a cultural novice's question: How is it that Americans can have a fistfight one minute and remain friends later?

Was there a worldly, free-spirited person hidden behind the dogged mien of a petite capitalist? I am not sure. Yet, I had seen that side of him that was curious and imaginative. At any rate, it was easy to root for my father and his plan. The wholesale had been planned to boost our financial future; we would one day be free from the long working hours and the lean take at the counter each day. It was a financial future that a child could expect from his or her shopkeeper father. And I am moved by the fact that the wholesale business had revealed many things I didn't know about him: his cleverness, his strategic bent, his bold economic vision. Still, my mother had made her point that the world is full of uncertainties, and it punishes the reckless. But even she, like the rest of family, had got swept away by my father's keenness and the infectious hope he invested in the new venture.

It is hard to forget the rural stores and their isolation and their makeshift look. You felt their impermanency, as if they were waiting out their final days before a new highway would run through and erase them from the landscape. My feeling towards the rural shops was mixed. They were our customers who sustained the wholesale business. But they had a way of reflecting my sense of insecurity. I thought: if things didn't work out at the High Street shop, we would be reduced to eking out a living in the countryside, like our rural customers. We would become the weary men and women whose shops were no more than grass huts. We wanted to make money from them, but we did not want to be like them. And they were to catch us off guard. We did not think they could be difficult—that they would not pay up for the trust and goodwill we had invested in them.

Over time, we noted the changes and not all for the worse. Some would close down, but others would expand and carry a wider range of goods. To these shops, the rural folks would walk the distance to buy what they needed, and consult the storekeeper about their discomforts and ailments. The storekeeper-cum-doctor was cheap, a cure for a sore back or a headache or a mild rheumatism costing only a few ringgit. Then one or two stores sprung up, offering the same merchandise and health services, and squeezed out the smaller ones. Social change and the new market were choosing a new set of winners and losers.

In the nineteen-seventies, Malaysia joined the four Asian Tiger economies—South Korea, Hong Kong, Taiwan and Singapore—and became the fifth tiger. The country was moving from mining and agriculture to manufacturing and services. Rubber and tin, for many years the mainstay of the economy, no longer dominated. The export-oriented economy laid the ground for the industrial growth of the eighties, based on heavy manufacturing with Japanese investment.[4] They brought about big structural changes, and urban growth began to push into the countryside. We noted the traffic conditions—the new busyness on the roads. Lorries were plying the roads and getting to the remote shops; the buses were picking up the routes previously deemed unprofitable. And the buses had improved on the old method. With the goods they made their journey with the passengers. On approaching the shop the driver pressed the horn, and the conductor would step down with the goods and got the shopkeeper to sign the receipt. There was no more hurling the package to the shop-front—like a paperboy on a suburban run in the West—as in the past.

The new villages of the counterinsurgency were becoming small town-ships and businesses rushed in to meet their needs. Those city wholesalers that had been serving the area expanded and picked up new clientele. On the main streets, coffee shops sprang up and became the town's meeting place and communication centre. People would go there to make calls for a small fee. Through the crackling landlines, they talked, and they gos-siped and haggled with those on the other end. For the young the high-light was the cinema showing kung fu movies—Bruce Lee was the rage. And there were smoky karaoke bars staffed by Thai women on visitor's visas. The nightlife was lifted from its customary stupor.

As the rural economy grew, so did the retail market stimulated by peo-ple with new purchasing power. It was a heady time for everyone, if less so for us. City wholesalers began to move in on the rural shops, our tradi-tional customers. As if imitating us, they used lorries and buses and when quick personal deliveries were asked for, their own vans. As business grew, they began to do what we could not afford: they purchased lorries and cut out the transport companies altogether. The big wholesalers were swoop-ing in on our market.

At the High Street shop we were still thinking that we were the pioneer, we had the first foot in the door. We had served these remote shops at a time when no one was interested in them. They had trusted us; these shops and stores were our domain.

We were comfortable in our belief, feeling smug that we had a hold on the people we enjoyed long-standing relationships with. But the economy and its social setting were changing. For those with an eye to see, the signs were clear. The traffic and the lorries and the buses, the telephone and, soon, television, the quickening pace of life—they suggested a major shift of the sleepy rural region; it was aligning itself with the encroaching forces from the city. The telephone had made people feel less isolated. And with better transport Kuala Lumpur was no longer out of reach as it used to be. When shop owners needed to make new orders, or to sort out a wrong delivery, they made a call or took a trip to the city. The horizon was opening up for the country storekeepers.

The indications were faint but perceptible. Perhaps we became aware of them when the customers turned peevish and made the kind of demands they would not make before. They complained that the goods they had received did not match the order; they were not happy with the prices charged on the invoice. And they rang and cancelled an order they had made barely a day or two ago. The humble compliant Hakka kinfolk had turned bothersome. My father wrote with his usual evasiveness: My son, I hope you are well. The wholesale business needs some adjustment, but nothing to worry about. The 'nothing to worry about' troubled me. At the college common room, I read and reread the letter, trying to nose out what was behind those words, those lines written by father's sturdy hands.

One summer I returned to witness first-hand the trouble brewing.

We were travelling to visit my father's old friend and customer Ah Lau. I was at the driver's seat and my father talked to fill me in. Hong Fatt Store still welcomed the salesman when he turned up, but its orders were smaller, more prudent. Ah Lau was coy and careful with his money. At the shop Ah Lau and his wife danced their ritual of greeting. Tea and groundnuts were served, and in return we gave compliment to their good health and the shop's prosperity evident in the slow, steady flow of customers. The Laus demurred: We are not worthy, please don't embarrass us.

This is what happens in the human economy. Each transaction is a soft shuffle of courtesy and thoughtfulness, but strategic intents lurk behind them. We had come to collect on a three-month-old invoice, and to take a fresh order if we were lucky. Ah Lau was equally judicious. He was similarly insistent—on not wanting to pay up.

Like other shop owners, Ah Lau was not insensible to what was happening at the High Street shop. For a while the boss had been sick, which required him to spend time in the hospital; everyone knew that. Over a month or so the shop was without a boss; my mother had taken over but it's not the same with a woman in charge. And news leaked out that after getting discharged from the hospital the boss was frequently tired and exhausted, which explained the mistakes in the invoices and delay in the deliveries. His first son was working elsewhere, and the others were overseas. Any sensible person would say: What a folly to pay one's debt to a business that was clearly on its last legs. It sounded like disloyalty, a betrayal of the guanxi sentiment that props up the artifice of Chinese petite capitalism.

However, it was nothing personal, as they say. The whole opportunity structure was shifting. It made people reassess their customary relationships and economic ties. They had not totally abandoned their alliances, but the temptation for disloyalty and for changing suppliers was great. Still, that's the trouble with doing business with kin: you couldn't simply discard them when you no longer find them useful. The large wholesalers meant more choices, better pricing—compared to the likes of the High Street shop. Rural retailers like Ah Lau could not respond to opportunities like the textbook economic rationalist. He dallied and tried to find a way out. Abandoning the High Street shop would probably make him a social pariah in the small circle of Hakka medicine traders, but he was not sure. There was the thought: what if the new supplier didn't work out; how could I then go back to Boss Yao who had helped to set me up and delivered the first order to fill the shelves?

So it's better the devil you know than the devil you don't. As with many of our rural customers, Ah Lau's relationship with us could be described as existing in half-suspension. He had kept us as his supplier, but meanwhile he was looking elsewhere. He dealt with us, and he dealt with other suppliers. We had a sense that he was moving on.

Thus, my father pressured and cajoled. With Ah Lau, the aim was not to retain his business but to collect the debt. It was a lot of work, and Ah Lau would stall our every effort. The driver-delivery man returned empty-handed, and only my father's actual presence made him cough up the small amount. Each of my father's visits produced the payment of a couple of hundred ringgit out of the standing debt of 7,500 ringgit. After my father died, one of my first tasks since I came back was to visit the country shops to see if I could collect from those who owed us. It was a forlorn and futile task. At Hong Fatt Store, I remember, Ah Lau had gone behind the counter and retrieved a bundle of notes from a metal tin box. I looked at them in my hand: they were a couple of twenty-ringgit bills. Was it meant to be an insult? This must be it: now the boss had died, so there was no need to take the son too seriously. The High Street shop would be closed soon; it was stupid to pay. Ah Lau murmured something about how good it was to have the boss' son back. But I didn't linger to hear the rest. I left and walked back to our my ever-reliable VW Kombi.

Ah Lau and his behaviour were typical. In more and more cases, other shops had delayed their payments or dished out a miserable amount. I was impatient. Everyone was half-minded about their decisions. The wholesale business was dragging on. I wanted to close it down straightaway and that meant getting back most of the debts owed to us. My mother said: people were giving face to your father, so they had paid whatever they could. You mustn't blame them. The wholesale was collapsing, but the social dealings persisted. It was messy, it was bad business practice.

The relationship between the rural stores and their supplier went awry because of the changing circumstances, because the basis of inter-personal trust had altered. But it is also true that people had, in different ways, believed in their own fiction—fiction about guanxi, about the trusting relationship they had enjoyed with each other. The rules of transaction were full of subterfuge. Their meanings were cryptic, and people abided to them as often as they defy and go against them. This was the situation facing the rural shops: they had stayed with the High Street shop, but they had also left themselves plenty of room for manoeuvre. The wholesale business in rural Malaysia was much like the peasant market everywhere: it was structurally complex, it was in tune with the prevailing cultural norms and it was 'so imbedded in its sociocultural context as to escape the reach of modern economic analysis altogether'.[5]

The remark comes from the anthropologist Clifford Geertz in his study of the traditional bazaar in Sefrou, Morocco. Similar to the situation in rural Malaysia, at the Sefrou bazaar each trader is tied to his customers in an on-going relationship. And here, too, the general principle applies: the trader wants to buy cheap (from the supplier) and sell dear, and the customers want to purchase goods of the right quality at the right price. Both want to get the most out of a transaction but freewheeling hard bargaining is constrained. Both aim to maximize gain, but the rules of sociality are not recklessly abandoned. What happens is typical of the traditional market where customary ties and relationships hold sway.

To buy and sell in the Sefrou bazaar, traders and customers need information that helps them to make the right decisions. For the traders, this is about building their 'market positions': a set of interweaving links with their customers and their fellow traders. However, what information is available is roughshod and full of hearsay. In Geertz's words, the information is 'poor, scarce, maldistributed, inefficiently communicated', yet it is 'intensely valued'.[6] Geertz describes the paradox.

> Neither the rich concreteness or reliable knowledge that the ritualized character of nonmarket economy makes possible, nor the elaborate mechanisms for information generation and transfer upon which industrial ones depend,

> are found in the bazaar: neither ceremonial distribution nor advertising; neither prescribed exchange partners nor product standardization. The level of ignorance about everything from product quality and going prices to market possibilities and product costs is very high, and much of the way in which the bazaar functions can be interpreted as an attempt to reduce such ignorance for someone, increase for someone, or defend someone against it.[7]

In Sefrou bazaar what people know about a product, or the personal qualities of the seller, is not great; yet they are not ignorant. As with our rural storekeepers, the traders in the Sefrou bazaar rely on teahouse gossips and the social grapevine. However, whatever information they can get is good enough to be useful. For them what is important is not true reliable information, but information that can be massaged and reconfigured to arrive at a version that would enable them to trade in the bazaar. Geertz describes such information as 'known ignorances'.[8]

The traders and the customers are bound by their relationship. And given what goes around the bazaar and beyond, they can't help knowing something of each other and the goods they are dealing with. In such a transaction the price and quality of a particular good, and the trader's capital and reputation are knowable. And these 'known ignorances' foster a buyer-seller relationship that is reasonably firm and lasting. In the bazaar, customers commit themselves to 'repetitive purchasers of particular goods and services' and 'the purveyors of them', 'rather than search widely through the market at each occasion of need'.[9] Each tries to stay loyal to the other. A degree of stability prevails—more or less.

All this is remarkably similar to the rural market which our wholesale business had once dominated. Here the wholesaler and the customers too operated in the half-light where trust and distrust, loyalty and betrayal, revealed themselves. If I have veered towards the fact of the rural storekeepers' moral frailty, Geertz brings our understanding back to the structural features of the traditional market. In my thinking, the rural market was full of uncertainty. Few things were pegged down; there were always last minute changes to orders people had made. The prices of goods had been set down on the invoice, but phone calls came to make a last pitch at bargaining. There were requests to have the goods delivered at another time—because, we suspected, the buyer was short of cash, or he was searching for another supplier. If the Sefrou bazaar traders rely on information which Geertz calls 'known ignorances', our rural retailers were 'indecisive decision-makers', striving for the midway between hard bargaining and compromises.

In Graeber's human economy, gracious social consideration is the rule. But social life is full of the less happy aspects. Bad faith, perfidy and double-dealing, too, take up residence in an imperfect world. The talk of 'our Hakka way of doing things' was tenacious between my father and his customers. In this talk, culture is hardened. Culture is the stuff of ancestral connections and communal solidarity. But it is also true that in the petite-capitalist world, honesty and trustworthiness tend to operate in half-measures.

Schumpeter has been described as 'a rarity', 'an economist with a tragic sense of life'.[10] His view of capitalism is dynamic and evolutionary. On capitalism's culture, he writes: '[capitalism] means a scheme of values, an attitude toward life, a civilization – civilization of inequality and of the family fortune.' And he reminds us, '[A] part of this capitalist culture is the fact of ever evolving, ever changing technology and method of production; old ways are left behind as the new and the more efficient are brought forward.'[11] In short, destruction is built into capitalism's revolution and innovation; it is a part of capitalism's inner logic. His idea of creative destruction shares with the Marxist notion of destruction as a natural process in capitalism's evolution and renewal.[12] Reading his *Capitalism, Socialism, and Democracy*, it is hard to ignore the fateful element—the play of inevitability—he gives to capitalism's onrush to revolutionize itself from within.

> [I]n capitalist reality as distinguished from its textbook picture, it is not [textbook] ... competition which counts but the competition from the new commodity, the new technology, the new source of supply, the new type of organization (the largest-scale unit of control for instance) – competition which commands a decisive cost or quality advantage and which strikes not at the margins of the profits and the outputs of the existing firms but at their foundations and their very lives.[13]

The one who sets this process in motion is the entrepreneur. The entrepreneur is an innovator. He is the Prometheus-like figure who tears down the old wisdoms and practices and heralds in the new—and gets punished for it.

I think of my parents: they dreamt the capitalist dream, a dream that promises much just as often as it fails to deliver. Schumpeter's notion of the entrepreneur, Arthur Miller's *The Death of a Salesman*, and the life of any of the storekeepers in rural Malaysia all suggest this.

Yet the question is often raised by the Chinese petite capitalist: I have the necessary virtues and business sense, why has success passed me by? Or: What have I done to deserve Heaven's wrath that has devastated my life and economic plan? In one way, my father's wholesale venture has been a mistake. He had misjudged the market and the investment needed to get wholesale up and running. That is true. But like all good petite capitalists, he strived for economic independence and that means grasping one's destiny in one's own hands, so to speak. Yet, greater forces were at play that brought about a catastrophe that no amount of hard work and frugality could head off. The failure of the wholesale business not only proved that it was a bad business decision, it was also a rebuke to the Chinese petite capitalist's customary brilliance.

My father comes across to me as a tragic figure, not because his petite-capitalist dream had failed him, but because the wholesale trade had taken himself to a moral universe that has its own logic and that dictates human affairs in its own terms.

Aristotle spoke of *peripeteia*, the reversal of circumstances as we have perceived and lived by them. The essence of tragedy is paradox: we have our own needs and legitimate desires, but destiny or fate has other plans. For the Greeks, the most tragic thing is when human design—for love, for wealth, for redemption—turns to ashes because the gods will otherwise. Willy Loman is, in this sense, tragic because his dream of getting ahead in capitalist America is destined to founder to begin with.

For Schumpeter, capitalism is innovative, as it moves towards ever greater efficiency and productivity. This positive force is also capitalism's inherent flaw. His famous concept 'creative destruction' embodies this double-faced quality of capitalist production. To destroy is to produce, to produce must entail a good deal of destruction of the old and the archaic and the inefficient.

This has a lot of resonance with Chinese petite capitalism. Chinese merchants are full of practicality and in-your-face pragmatism. Even virtue and a person's character can be useful. And this practicality and pragmatism Chinese petite capitalists consider the main reason for their business successes. If this is innovation, it—to borrow a few lines from Schumpeter—'does not essentially consist in either inventing anything or otherwise creating the conditions which the enterprise exploits. It consists in getting things done.'[14]

In the final analysis, no one was to be blamed for the collapse of my father's wholesale business—neither the big city suppliers nor us nor the rural shops. They were all Willy Lomans and their acts and wishes were aborted by forces more mysterious, more unpredictable, than they could imagine. In the hard grind of petite capitalism, personal action and economic wisdom matter little in the long run. The winners today would be the losers tomorrow, and new comers would enter in the endless cycle of change and renewal.

## Notes

1. Joseph Schumpeter, *Capitalism, Socialism and Democracy.* New York: Harper & Row, 1950.
2. Ibid., p. 132.
3. Souchou Yao. *The Malayan Emergency.* Copenhagen: NIAS Press, 2016.
4. Jomo K.S. *Growth and Structural Change in the Malaysian Economy.* London: Palgrave Macmillan, 1990, p. 38.
5. Clifford Geertz, 'The Bazaar Economy: Information and Search in Peasant Marketing', *The American Economy Review* 68 (2), 1978, p. 28.
6. Ibid., p. 29.
7. Ibid.
8. Ibid.
9. Ibid., p. 30
10. Daniel Bell, *The Cultural Contradictions of Capitalism.* New York: Basic Books, 1976, p. 178.
11. Joseph Schumpeter. *Capitalism, Socialism and Democracy*, p. 52.
12. The idea of destruction as capitalism's inner logic is dispersed over Marx's work. An apocalyptic version is given in The Communist Manifesto where he and Engels wrote: 'It is enough to mention the commercial crises that by their periodical return put the existence of the whole of bourgeois society on trial, each time more threateningly. In these crises, a great part not only of existing production, but also of previously created productive forces, are periodically destroyed.' 'Manifesto of the Communist Party', in *The Portable Karl Marx*, edited by Eugene Mamenka, New York: Viking Penguin, 1983, p. 210.
13. Joseph Schumpeter. *Capitalism, Socialism and Democracy*, p. 82
14. Ibid., p. 132.

## Bibliography

Bell, Daniel. 1976. *The Cultural Contradictions of Capitalism.* New York: Basic Books.

Geertz, Clifford. 1978. 'The Bazaar Economy: Information and Search in Peasant Marketing'. *The American Economy Review* 68 (2): 28-32.

Jomo K.S. 1990. *Growth and Structural Change in the Malaysian Economy.* London: Palgrave Macmillan.

Marx, Karl and Frederic Engels, 'Manifesto of the Communist Party', in *The Portable Karl Marx*, edited by Eugene Mamenka, New York: Viking Penguin, 1983, pp. 203-241.

Schumpeter, Joseph. 1950. *Capitalism, Socialism and Democracy.* New York: Harper & Row.

Yao, Souchou. 2016. *The Malayan Emergency.* Copenhagen: NIAS Press.

CHAPTER 9

# Family Legacy

When my father passed away, my family did not tell me the news. I was then in Adelaide completing the last year of an Economics degree. The news reached me through a friend who had just returned from Malaysia. Twelve months later I returned home after finishing my studies. My mother, comforted by having her favourite son with her, tried to bring up the subject. She didn't know what to do, she said. Everything was in a chaos. She knew I was in the middle of my exam and she wanted to shield me from the sad news. Then she started to cry. Your poor father, he had worked so hard all his life, always thinking about the family, about how to save up to give all of you an education. Your poor father, such a bitter life he had lived. Her words clasped at my breast, lugging me into her majestic unhappiness. I have come back, I said to her. Everything will be all right. You don't want to get sick from worrying.

For many years on, I often dreamed about my father. In the dreams he was sitting behind the counter, his round face grave with concentration, his left hand pressing the phone to the ear and his right-hand fingers running over the abacus. His mouth moved as he spoke, but no words came out. The unconscious has its own logic. Since I—since it—could not accept my father's death, he came alive in my dreams. I remember the exhilaration of these dreams. 'Seeing' my father in person steeped in his daily routines calmed my panic. He was again in charge. Everything would be put right. The family would still be the bastion of love and security it



S. Yao, *The Shop on High Street*,
https://doi.org/10.1007/978-981-15-2031-0_9

had always been. The torn threads of our lives would be restrung. I woke up in tears, filled with self-pity.

Father's death left many things to be sorted out. We needed to wind down the High Street shop, and to find the money to support my younger brother Paul still in Adelaide doing a Pharmacy degree. My elder brother had been looking after the family business since our father died; he was about to migrate to Australia with his family. Everything now fell on my shoulders. A few months ago my life was one of crowded lecture rooms and beer-sodden student parties; now I faced the dusty account ledgers and creditors and suppliers wanting to get paid. I was hauled back to a familiar world now without my father. And without him, the family business was as a rudderless boat, going nowhere. The High Street shop was nothing without him.

At the solicitor's office, we—my mother, my sisters and I—gathered to listen to Mr Tan as he read out the will. There was not much in the way of inheritance. We had gone through the books that revealed the family's financial position. The shop had been heavily mortgaged; it would be sold to pay off the bank. The small terrace house my parents had bought for retirement would go to my mother. Then there were the savings people had deposited in the shop and my father's personal loans. These deposits and loans had plugged the holes of emergencies, and they had kept the wholesale trade running right until my father's death. There were pieces of jewellery my father had bought for my younger sister's education fund; they should be kept for that purpose. The will was sparse and matter-of-fact. We the children would look after our mother, and we must see our young sister through school and support her education.

I asked Mr Tan how to handle the debts. He said that the depositors had to be paid at a percentage to be worked out. But the personal loans—each scribbled on a flimsy chit of paper, some not even signed—we could probably get away with not paying. He was being formal and legalistic. An LSE (London School of Economics) man, with a clerkship at Gray's Inn, he knew little about the customary obligations that operate in the Chinese business world, or so I thought. As soon as people had found out about the shop's closure, I said to him, everyone would be coming and demanding their money back. But he assured me he had dealt with similar cases before; he was aware of the furies of debtors unpaid.

A few months later, we convened a creditors' meeting at a rented school hall in the city. Let us get a big room, Mr Tan had said. We must be prepared; things might get a bit rowdy. Some fifty men and women eventually turned up; many I had known since childhood. They milled about in little groups and talked among themselves. Waiting for more to arrive, Mr Tan and I retreated to the backroom. I tried to psych myself up for the meeting. Mr Tan looked at me and gave me a nudge: It'll okay, trust me. I smiled meekly, thinking: from a student's life to overseeing the closing of the family shop—it was a shortcut to adulthood and responsibility. The shop had been our home, our livelihood, and my mind was full of the dregs of unresolved feelings: the regret about the shop's demise, the guilt for not being at home when my father died, the suspicion that I had somehow failed my parents.

We went back to the school hall and sat behind the podium made up of two school desks. Before us rows of faces stared back at us with their piqued, angry eyes. Mr Tan made a brief speech. He asked the creditors to be patient. He assured them all debts, big and small, would be repaid. After the meeting they must come forward with their passbooks and letters, and we would jot down the details. He was to represent them and look after their interests. The debts would be paid at 25 sen to a ringgit, he announced. It would be fair, and what the family could afford, he told them.

A voice came from the back and cut in on Mr Tan. Loud and clear, it hit at us at the podium. You have to pay back all the money, it said. The father's debt is the son's debt! Then it paused as though for effect. When it resumed it was to issue a warning: You watch it. If you don't pay back, you may never walk the street again. The mood was changed and the crowd, as though in cue, cried out: The father's debt is the son's debt! You have to pay up!

I was stung by the bellicose turn of the meeting. I was taken aback. I was astounded. Were these the people whom I had been taught to call Uncles and Aunties since I was a child? Were these our kith and kin who drank tea with our parents, who brought us sweets and lucky money during Chinese New Year? People stood up, waved their hands as though in a political rally. The meeting was descending into chaos. No doubt they were justified in their rage, but all I could think of was: Would they really send some ruffians to roughen us up in some alleyway at night? Would they really?

The leading voice had come from Iron Monger Lee, my father's old friend. He had appointed himself the leader of the crowd. I had not seen him for a few years but I remembered his makeshift wide-eyed look and his dusty face; apart from the hair gone peppery grey, nothing much had changed. There he was: my father's financier, the man who taught me the 'horse-shitting stance' of Chinese kung fu. And I remembered, too, that we were almost made in-laws. When his daughter Grace decided to enrol in the Economics Department at Adelaide University where I had been for two years, my father had written to me: Grace is your Uncle Lee's daughter; you know her and you must look after her. I had met her through family meetings, but we were not close. The day she arrived, I picked her up from the airport and took her to lunch. I helped her to find a room in a shared-house and introduced her to my friends. A pretty, vivacious young woman, she soon settled in and made friends of her own. So I left her to her charmed social circles. One day a sour letter came from my father: your Uncle Lee said that you have been neglecting young Grace; he said you have not been looking after her. It took a while for the idea to sink in. The hints were all there, but I was blind to them. There had been an attempt at matchmaking and I had somehow spoiled it. At any rate here he was—a family friend and co-plotter of my marital future, demanding his money back and calling for blood.

The parleying with the creditors continued. They rang and they came to the shop and demanded their money. The shop had ceased trading, and I thought it best that my mother and the rest of the family should move out and I would stay on. In any case I craved time on my own, and thought it better that they settle in the small terrace house we had bought years ago. For almost six months before the business finally closed, I together with Uncle Low, an old worker of ours, became the caretaker. I spent my time reading and writing longingly to the friends I had left behind. People came to the shop and I received them in the best way I could. They should contact Mr Tan, I told them. He was handling the affair, not I. In spite of myself, I felt sorry for them—the men and women who had put their money into the High Street shop. Free from Iron Monger Lee's incitement, they turned meek and diffident. They were not wealthy; they had saved hard and they had trusted their savings to us. Away from the fiery creditors' meeting, their plight had become more real to me.

Looking back, I do not begrudge the days when I held the fort at the shop. I felt alone—old Uncle Low was not much of a company, but it turned out to be an interesting time for me. With the affair of the shop unsettled I could not look for a job. I was left with plenty of time on my hands. I went through the books I brought back and finished reading what I had started at the university: R.H. Tawney's *Religion and the Rise of Capitalism*, E.P. Thompson's *The Making of the English Working Class*, as well as the works of Orwell and Conrad. I saw *Bonnie and Clyde* in a midnight screening in the Rex Cinema in Petaling Street, and was stung by the violence that marked the new Hollywood. After the movie it was pleasant to walk through the empty streets at two in the morning, the city cool and all but shut down.

Once a month or so, I had lunch with Mr Tan at the Selangor Club. I was getting to like the man who was formal and practical, cynical about the follies of human affairs. After lunch we went back to his office where we tried to sort out a few things. I helped him to go through my father's papers and ledgers for some bits of information he needed. And he gave me the letters I needed to sign. The first round of letters had been sent out, but many were returned to the office marked 'Undelivered'. Perhaps people had lost interest as the matter dragged on, or perhaps it was hard for the post to reach the huts and the tin-roofed houses in the remote villages where some of the creditors lived. Mr Tan made some joke about the best way not to pay a debt is to delay, and let people wait until they lose interest and drop out. It was a joke of questionable taste, I said, but secretly I took note of what it meant.

Some of my father's associates proposed that we children should carry on our father's business. They would put together a package, they said, to pay the debts and restart the business. They thought the shop would make money if it was properly managed. And they said as encouragement: Your father had taken over from his father, and now you'll take over from yours. I listened to their proposal; all I could think of was how it would benefit them. They were our major creditors; the ledger showed we owed them altogether nearly 250,000 ringgit. It was a simple financial ruse: to keep alive the business was to keep alive the debts, and they would recoup the money when the time was right, when the shop began to do well. But then they could also be thinking about the family. Perhaps as our kin and my father's long-time friends, they wanted to keep alive his good name, his legacy. It would be the right thing to do for the descendants of any middle-class family.

I discussed the proposal with my family. No one took it seriously. The talk of legacy troubled me—almost as much as the creditors' threat and anger. The idea of legacy brought up many things I did not want to think about. I had finished university, I was an adult now and certain claims could be made on me regarding my responsibility towards the family. In my mind, though, whatever plans I had for myself, they did not include living and working again in the High Street shop. Of that I was sure—even when I had yet decided what I wanted to do, where I would eventually settle. In any case, save for a few exceptional years, the High Street shop had not made money. It was touch and go financially. Whatever the people said, it made no sense to revive the business. None of us—my mother, we siblings—wanted that.

Legacy is a difficult issue for anyone. Apart from anything else, it is designed to make claims on you in all kinds of ways. Legacy is like the blood that flows through your veins: both carry deposits of your ancestry, your origin, and something of your parents that has become a part of you. A certain moral obligation is imposed on you. For the wealthy, legacy is largely about money and property and business. Who can argue against the logic of taking over what the parents have achieved and bringing it to even greater glory and profitability? The pressure of inheritance hovers over everyone in the family. You need a touch of unhappy childhood, a measure of rebelliousness, to see through the sanctity of it all. As for Chinese patrimony, it feels at times the deceased have reached out their deadly hands and staked a claim on the living.

Our relatives had proposed that we take over the shop, but we had other plans for ourselves. We wanted to have our career choices, but we knew we had to sort out our obligations towards our parents—towards our father's legacy. I am sure my parents did not think about this: that sending us to the university overseas would change us in many ways. We could not have spent those years away in a foreign place only to come back and pick up where we had left off. University education had made my brothers and I disloyal. It had granted us a modern profession, and a life-style against which the High Street shop was a poor competitor.

Yet, when I think this aloud, it sounds brash and only half true. For the decision facing us was not simply between what we wanted for ourselves and what we owed to the family. The idea of legacy left us with a bundle of mixed feelings, and crammed our minds with guilt.

In a way we had seen it coming. It could not be said that father's death was unexpected. He was rarely sick in his younger years, but in his mid-forties he was diagnosed with diabetes and high blood pressure. Results of stress and overwork, the doctor had said. Later he was admitted to the Lady Templer's Hospital for the early stages of tuberculosis. The month's stay at the sanatorium was a peaceful time for him. Free from the phone calls and the work at the shop, he rested and even put on weight. During our visits we found him strolling at the hospital ground, or resting on the bed reading his papers and going through the account books he couldn't resist bringing. They were images of well-being I keep still in my memory. The doctor was optimistic when he discharged his patient. He thought my father's health could be managed by regular consultation and prescribed medication. He was to eat well; he was to do exercise and take time off whenever he could. At home my mother cooked him ginseng soup and steamed bird's nest with rock sugar—medicines that foster the qi and nourish the lungs. After I got my driver's licence, we—I, my youngest sister, our parents—started to drive to the Lake Gardens every Sunday morning. For a few hours, we forgot the shop, and my mother and I sat under the shade and watched the perfect scene of father and daughter at play. We drank our Coke, while they went over to the lake with their bags of stale bread for the ducks. They held on to each other, and moving closer to the water's edge, strewed the bread pieces over the water, then stepped back to watch the feeding frenzy.

My father's illnesses were a key story of the High Street shop. We didn't struggle with them much as we treated them as an element of our daily living, things we accepted and learned to cope with. After my father's discharge from the hospital, we buckled down and made a few changes to make his life comfortable. We installed a telephone upstairs so he could take the calls there; we did the Sunday morning drives to the Lake Gardens; we got him to take time off and go to the movie with us once a week. And he took a lot of self-prescribed Chinese medicine—ginseng and beef broth, bird's nest soup or dessert of ginkgo seeds. In the kitchen I often sat with a bowl of the herbal soup to keep him company while we talked.

My father carried on the best he could. But in many ways, life imperceptibly changed for him and his family. A bridge was built between the 'kingdom of the well' and the 'kingdom of the sick', to use Susan Sontag's memorable phrases.[1] I remember when I went to fill his insulin prescription, his old friend Mr Mohamed the pharmacist would ask about him: 'How is your father? Get him to take time off, that's the main thing.' He was voicing what we all knew: taking time off from work mattered as much as the medications and the insulin shots. Sometimes when his condition made a turn for the worse, one of our relatives would come and help in the shop. They were old friends and kin, and having retired from their own businesses had plenty of time on their hands. And their presence lifted the gloom at the shop and cheered us up. When my father died, it was these men and women who gathered around his widow—an army of consolers who took over one of the final affairs of the High Street shop, my father's funeral.

Susan Sontag writes:

> Illness is the night-side of life, a more onerous citizenship. Everyone who is born holds dual citizenship, in the kingdom of the well and in the kingdom of the sick. Although we all prefer to use only the good passport, sooner or later each of us is obliged, at least for a spell, to identify ourselves as citizens of that other place.' … [I]llness is not a metaphor … Yet it is hardly possible to take up one's residence in the kingdom of the ill unprejudiced by the lurid metaphors with which it has been landscaped.[2]

Sontag speaks of cancer and tuberculosis (TB). We knew about TB—not only from our father's illness. We had heard of the dreadful disease from relatives in China, and from the lorry drivers who came and bought bulk streptomycin to send back to their villages. Susan Sontag is right. Wellness and sickness may divide us, but healthy or ill we are forced to deal what lies at the other place over the border. No one—except the romantic and the hypochondriac—wants to take up residence in the kingdom of the ill. Still, as I write my mind is filled with fantasies and thoughts that put us under the spell of that strange geography. In Thomas Mann's *The Magic Mountain*, a TB sanatorium becomes a place of knowledge and self-discovery. Illness tends to figure as a metaphor, as a set of meaning.

When I look back, my father's death comes back to me with its awful finality. In the kingdom of the deceased, everything about him—his goodness, his over-stretch in the pursuit of the capitalist dream—came to an end. His death was devastating, but more so his long intermitting period of illness.

Throughout the period of illness, he was able to work. But the most serious illness took place over the last six months of his life; but they felt longer. He was in and out of hospital, and my mother had written and kept me informed. For my brother and I, it was an unspoken question: should we leave our studies and go back? The letter from home said he was fine, and there was no need for worry. Eventually a practical sense won over, and we stayed on to finish our studies. He died, and I had not kept vigilance at the hospital bed during his final hours. I was not home for his funeral. The realization played on my mind, and sent me to a wretchedness of guilt. And each time I think of my father, it brings me back to the time at home when I sat with him and helped him with the injection.

Projected on the screen of my mind, the images.

I take the injection kit from my father, light the spirit burner and boil the set of syringe and needle over the flame. He is tired, and he slumps back at the sofa. Seeing him waiting makes me pick up the pace. The injection kit needs only a few seconds of boiling. I fill the syringe from an insulin ampoule, then against the light, tap it to expel the air inside. I am playing nurse: I know any air bubble would be fatal, and the shot is to be made at the leg muscle. My father takes the syringe from my hand and makes his shot. A red nipple of a swelling rises on the skin. The patient lies back, and I move closer and press a finger to hold down the swelling. I look at him: he is exhausted, in near coma; he breathes softly, his eyes drooping. I am up-close with my father and his illness. I feel the depth of sympathy. In my head the idea—a set of questions—comes to me: Would he ever get well? What would happen to us if he never recovers from his illnesses? I am stumped by the questions which have more to do with us than with my father. They are unworthy of me; they have risen from the fear of abandonment. The kingdom of the ill is no longer a foreign country, but one that implicates us deeply.

My father's funeral was a grand affair, people told me. Since my younger brother and I were not at home, my mother had employed a photographer to make a record of the proceedings. The photo album shows a burial ritual meticulously observed, so my anthropologist's eye tells me. Picture after picture, scene after scene, the photos show the gathering, the crowd outside the shophouse; my mother and siblings and close kin in black pants and brown hashan blouses, an austere outfit of mourning; the parade of mourners and well-wishers, led by an orchestra and gong players, ushering a black hearse weighed down with wreaths. Then shots of the burial party stopping at the foothill of the Cantonese Public Cemetery; the transfer of the coffin to a lighter van that travels up the path to the grave; the teary witnesses; the final burial and closing of the grave. The photographer had assembled the pictures in a meaningful order, like a film's mise-en-scène shot according to the script. It is as though he had set up the scenes for the camera, and the mourners, our relatives, my mother, my siblings were actors.

I flip back to the earlier pages. The wake was held inside the shop, and the priests and their assistants and the mourners had flowed from the shop onto the five-foot path outside. All day people came and burned incense to pay respect to the dead. At night, though, the place shed its gloom, livened up by people eating and playing mah-jong. This is the purpose of the wake: the dead need the cheery companionship of the living as they make the crossing to the underworld. There are many pictures of people eating and talking and having a good time, and I wonder if some of them are not hangers-on who have come for the supper and the 'lucky money'.

It was a grand affair, and it was expensive. Our relatives quite rightly thought my mother would be too distraught to attend to the details. They had taken over and had kept an account of the expenses. It made alarming reading when I saw it. The dinners for the night attendants and mourners costed 1,500 ringgit; the two priests were paid 200 ringgit each per day over three days, making a total of 1,200 ringgit. For the funeral parade, the 'red packet' lucky money for the orchestra and wreath holders and flag carriers came to some 4,000 ringgit. There were other expenses for flowers and incense and oil, the hiring of cars and lorries, and wages for the army of helpers. When we sat down to examine the accounts, my mother had put the blame on Second Uncle from Sungei Buloh. Second Uncle had taken charge, she said, everything was left to him. She was advised that things had to be done properly; her husband was the pillar of the community and we had to give him face. It was chaotic, with so many things to do and people to feed and entertain. So my mother just signed the cheques and took out the cash when people asked for it. What else was she to do?

The funeral was more extravagant than necessary. We are Hakka folk; it is not our habit to waste money and on such a scale. But then what would be a simpler, less expensive funeral like? There would still be the army of mourners, the priests and the night people who send my father off to the land of the dead. It was a funeral befitting of my father's social status. But all the money was spent which we could ill afford; it upset my petite bourgeoise sensibility. Still a funeral is held not only for the deceased, but also for the living. The net of participants had been cast wide for my father's burial. The priests and wreath carriers, the mourners and freeloaders, the relatives and friends who dropped in to pay their respects—they all had a place in it. We needed them to memorialize the man's life and many virtues. A person so distinguished should not be made to make the crossing alone to the nether world. The funeral had to be a public affair; it was to celebrate the legacy of the dead.[3]

Legacy matters to a family because of the built-in expectations it has about its own continuance. For the wealthy if less so for the poor, legacy is about the line of descent in which unmarried sons and daughters, and the married ones who bear no children, are a curse. The other concern is social and economic: how to ensure the forefather's name live on, and the wealth he has bestowed on the living would be maintained. Nothing spoils more the ancestor's legacy than the black sheep in the family who stays single and squanders the wealth and causes altercations. It is a universal story. Wealth and inheritance are the main issues, so are the burden and responsibility that legacy brings on the descendants. Legacy poses for them the fear of losing what has been bequeathed to them, the fear that they do not have the talent their forefathers had in building the family wealth. Legacy as a story of risk and disappointment—this is not often told.[4]

The Americans speak of 'from rags to riches to rags', the French say that 'it is easier to make money than to keep it,' the British bewail more graphically 'shirt-sleeves to shirt-sleeves in three generations' and for the Chinese it is 'great wealth can't last beyond three generations.'[5] They all depict a family's gloomy transition from prosperity to insolvency. And they cast blame on the descendants. I grew up with similar moral forewarnings. My father's version was, referring to a common Malaysian scene: a grandfather rides a bicycle to the office while his children and grandchildren drive around in their Hondas and Mercedes Benz sedans. Longevity, frugality and financial good sense are the legends much treasured by Chinese petite capitalists. And against these legends, the faults of the descendants are many. On the matter of legacy, there is no greater fault than frittering away the family inheritance.

The descendants' wastefulness and poor business sense is one thing; the other is the nature of the traditional Chinese inheritance law. In Europe—and Japan—primogeniture is the norm, a form of inheritance that passes on the family estate to the eldest son, though his male siblings are provided for. The advantage of the system is that it keeps whole the family estate, which eldest son alone owns and controls. The risk here is that so much is invested in a single offspring. When he fails, he brings down the whole family business. In contrast, the Chinese opt for equal inheritance among male descendants. Unlike primogeniture, the Chinese system has the virtue of equitability (among the sons). But the trouble with Chinese patrimony is that many sons are cutting into the same cake. Over time, as the number of descendants grows, each individual holding gets smaller. Unless each generation can increase the family wealth, the ancestral estate is put to risk by the never-ending divisions. There is another thing. With Chinese inheritance, the estate is shared but the control and management are in the hands of the senior male: the father or the eldest son, or both. For the younger sons, inheritance is not what it sounds. What they own is still formally managed by another in the family. Each of the younger sons has a share of the estate, but equitability does not describe it.[6] The seeds of discord and conflict are sown.

Over the years there have been attempts to paint a different picture of Chinese patrimony. Often customary law and actual practice do not match. Victor Zheng of Hong Kong University, in his 2000 study of family firms in Hong Kong, makes a singular observation. The study reveals that in post-British Hong Kong, equal distribution of family inheritance among sons is still the norm. However, the result is not as disastrous as it is commonly believed. As Zheng describes, as each son receives his share of the estate, he often uses it to branch out on his own. Each son has his own holding, which he controls and makes it grow. The practice leads to a healthy competition among the brothers, and the enterprises tend to create a consortium of sort. The consortium is loosely family-based, and each son enjoys a degree of autonomy within the overarching structure. The sons are separate economically, but the agnatic ties encourage the brothers to cooperate and lend each other support. In such a setup, a non-toxic friendly competition prevails.

> [T]he equal inheritance may weaken economic capital formation, but it doesn't affect human and social capital. Instead, it creates a base for sibling competition. Comparison generates psychological stress and anxiety. Such stress and anxiety will turn to competition. Competition is a driving force that motivates each members (sic) to work harder, and to excel over others. This driving force is called the "self-employment mentality". It is a spirit to free oneself from subjugation, to found one's own kingdom, and to prove that one is superior to other siblings.[7]

It is a dynamic situation that Zheng describes. The family-based consortium is not free from competition between the brothers. But they are keen to cooperate, egged on by their interest in keeping up the father's good name. At best, it is a system that allows the son to be somewhat heroically their own persons free from the father's—or the eldest brother's—overbearing authority.

In the will my father had, in a fashion, adhered to the Chinese customary law. The inheritance—the High Street shop business mainly—was to be shared among his sons. The two daughters received the jewellery which he had bought and hoarded over the years, and my mother was given the terrace house he had purchased for their retirement. It is not quite the formal system that Zheng describes. But my father had more or less followed the rule, and he had provided for the women in the family. Still, he had left things vague. His will said that my brothers and I would share the business, and left it at that. Did he had in mind that we should take up our professional jobs and somehow fit the herbal business into our working schedules? Did he mean that we should share the responsibility and keep the shop going? I quickly put the questions away. My father was a practical man. I truly believe that, having invested so much in our education, he would want us to strike out on our own and give up the shop. He would want to save us from the stress and the burden he and our mother had endured.

Chinese family inheritance is about wealth distribution; it is also about the family and its continuity. A family is 'where the cultural reproduction of the person that of the [family] are ... intertwined', the anthropologist George Marcus writes.[8] Cultural reproduction, in this sense, speaks of the transfer of things vital to the family and its members. Property inheritance provides the economic base, while passing on the intergeneration loyalty and values ensures the descendants would fit in their forefathers' mould. Our conventional thinking, however, has been to 'give a priority to the reality of collectivity over the unique, autonomous selves of the members."[9] Marcus has in mind the American family trust where the descendants' needs and aspirations are often neglected, while the family legacy is elevated. Across cultures and societies, the wrangling between individual needs and collective demands are not easily resolved. This is no less so in the Chinese family—despite the Confucian harmony that is allegedly its foundation. Here the descendants wonder about their obligations towards the dead, about the weight of inheritance and how to manage it. They may even ask as people everywhere ask when facing the question of legacy: What is in it for me?

The question was academic, as they say. We never went beyond playing with a certain idea. My younger brother Paul had stayed on to finish his Pharmacy degree, and before I left we talked about the future of the High Street shop. We were enticed by the idea: perhaps we could turn it into a mini-mart, with air-conditioning and neat rows of steel shelves and cabinets. The wooden boxes inserted into the wall and containing dried herbs and animal parts—they would have to go. We would deal only in patent medicine and herbal teas, sealed in vacuum packs and their contents visible. It would be a clean modern shop selling modern goods. And we would add new product lines: shampoos and conditioners, health drinks and slimming aids, cognac and whisky, besides the Tiger Balm and Brands

Essence of Chicken. It was quite a plan. But we were like two children acting out the fantasy of being adults, a pleasant game.

As we talked, the problem persisted in our minds. We knew we could never have our father's skill and perseverance. We would, if we were to take over the business, find daunting his world of deal making and bland materialism; the art of cut-throat competition was beyond us. Professor Zheng thinks that a father's social capital consists of 'leadership, personal ties and business networks', which are inherited by the son for his use.[10] But social capital is personal; it is attached to an individual. It is a fantasy to think one's 'leadership, personal ties and business networks' can be simply transferred from father to son. And I had discovered this in my dealings with our creditors: You cannot, by bearing your father's surname and by virtue of being his progeny, invite the same favours and considerations from his kith and kin as he could.

The 'cultural reproduction of the self' does not follow a single, harmonious path. It can be dramatic and conflictual that pits sibling against sibling, sons and daughters against parents, and it makes one want to break free from the family. Or it may leave one relatively untouched, as a son or daughter makes compromises and abides to the family demands. Most of us, though, find a middle way. Still, there are those who never manage. For them legacy intensifies the conflict, and the family becomes a battleground.

It is a cliché, yet it is often true. People leave home—to go to war, to travel, to get an education—and come back and carry on as before. Others return changed and feel out of sync with their previous lives. Of course, we can also feel the ground-shift by staying at home. Events that happen around us—social conflict and political unrest, the parents' divorce, a death in the family—can be similarly harrowing. For travellers and home-stayers alike, 'life is an adventure' rings true. It is Simmel who says: adventure is about 'dropping out of the continuity of life' yet deeply a part of it—a typical modern paradox.

> What we call an adventure stands in contrast to that interlocking of life-links, to that feeling that those counter-currents, turnings, and knots still, after all, spin forth a continuous thread ... Nevertheless ... [w]hile it falls outside the context of life, it falls with this same movement as it were, back into that context again ... it is a foreign body in our existence which is yet somehow connected with the center.[11]

Death in the family counts as an adventure in Simmel's sense—an extraordinary event and yet, if you survive it, a mere break in the flow of life. With a death in the family, you hold on to the memory of the deceased. You want to honour the life they had led. In mourning you commemorate their love and their virtues, you promise yourself you would try to live up to the examples they had set.

In Adelaide, when I heard the news of my father's passing, I wrote back and asked my mother to stop sending me money. I started looking for a part-time job. I planned to support myself. I wanted to pay my own way and relieve her from the financial burden.

The job I found was two evenings a week at the Chopsticks Restaurant on South Road, a dust-eaten strip of factories and used-car yards south of the city. Every Saturday and Sunday afternoon, from four o'clock to midnight, I stood before a wok of boiling oil and deep-fried pork pieces in batter for making the sweet-and-sour pork much favoured by the Australian customers. Over the wok, I also turned overripe bananas into banana fritters to be served with ice cream. It was greasy and grimy work. On a quiet night I would be asked to leave the kitchen and serve the tables at the dining room.

The scene at the dinner came straight from the photographer Weegee's pictures of New York City at night. There were taxi drivers dropping by for a break over a plate of dim sum and hot tea, smoking heavily at a time when smoking in a diner was allowed. There were policemen and policewomen who, after a day on the beat, stopped to pick up a pack or two of curry chopsuey, or sweet-and-sour duck, on their way home. At the corner table a middle-aged couple sipped their BYO ('bring-your-own') bottle of claret, holding hands and whispering sweet conspiracy like a scene from the film *The Postman Always Rings Twice*: was someone going to get done in so that the two could get another shot at happiness? I was among the night owls, with their tired droopy eyes and insomniac scheming. At the Chopsticks Restaurant, I slaved over the boiling wok, I served the tables and I washed and scrubbed the floor after closing. I was undeterred. A few weeks ago I was in the bear grip of depression, now I was deep in the practicalities of earning a living.

In my flat after work, I sat in the bathtub to wash away the grime and rewarded myself with a Vodka on ice. I felt enormously proud. I had not been lazy and a burden to the family. I had not skipped classes to work on my grief. I had kept a job at a greasy eating house when things at home were falling apart—indication enough for me that I was my father's son.

Chopstick Restaurant had given me the experience of dignified labour. At the High Street shop work was family labour, and with family labour you did not speak of pay or personal reward and significance. Work at the Chopstick Restaurant was different. The restaurant was run by a young Hong Kong couple, the Wangs, who employed Asian students for their company and for their cheap labour. I was a quick learner, and the husband and wife never had to give me firm instructions. I became an expert deep fryer within a week after starting. I did the job given to me; I enjoyed no favours or indulgence. All this I remember, and most sharply the first pay packet: the notes in the brown envelope felt justified, a true measure of the labour I had put in. Neither Mrs Wang nor I said thank you. There was no reason for gratitude for both employer and worker. Our relationship was objective and economically defined; it was free from the jumble of emotions.

It is bit of a shame that I should feel this way: that work and money figure large in one's idea of independence, as a measure of one's self-worth.

The author of 'The Adventure' also wrote *The Philosophy of Money*.[12] 'The levelling of objects to that of money reduces the subjective interest first in their specific qualities and then, as a further consequence, in the objects themselves', Simmel writes.[13] Money renders a commodity's value in unit parcels—five dollars' worth of apples, ten dollars' worth of oranges. Money-based exchange is modern economic exchange; it works by inserting itself in the chain between desire and its fulfilment, between what I need and how I go about meeting it. The exchange of equivalences—'one orange equates two apples'—that permeates economic life also means the flattening of what is certain and recognizable, giving social life and the relationships between people a certain fluidity. In Simmel's own words, commenting on the modern capitalist culture:

> All in all, one can say that the peculiar psychological coloration – or better, decoloration – to which things are subjected by their equivalence to a completely colourless means of exchange brings, as it were, a certain smoothness, a grinding down of their sharp corners and, by easing and accelerating the circulation of things in that way, this is a side of the cultural process which transforms both ideals and realities from the form of stability, something unchangeably fixed and existing forever, into that of motion, the eternal flow of things and continuous development.[14]

The money-driven modern culture is a paradox. It equalizes, it levels things out and it grinds down the sharp corners of diversity and differences.

On the other hand, it emphasizes individuality and supports personal independence; it permits autonomy and freedom.

The talk of money and the reward of working in the Chopstick Restaurant is typical petite bourgeoise sensibility. A shopkeeper's son, I could recognize what I had felt—the security of money, the thrill of earning it and work as a near heroic undertaking that gives life meaning. They had grown out of my existence at the High Street shop, a mixture of oppression and exhilaration. I did not choose to be the offspring of my parents. Yet their goodness and decency, my father's immoderation and driving ambition to make good had willy-nilly become mine. Drawing a wide arc, you begin to realize not only your parents and their values have made you, so have history and the social surroundings in which you have lived. I am thinking of the laundry-shop-and-chopsuey-houses Chinamen of the American racial stereotype, or the money-is-everything orang cina middleman traders in rural Malaysia. These figures came alive, in both countries, from the prejudices and the specific economic relations and government policies. In Malaya the colonial Divide-and-Rule had created the 'essential outsider' of the Chinese and Indian immigrants who laboured in the tin mines and plantations and took up much of the commercial sector, while the Malay indigene were holders of the traditional social order and deserved protection and political sponsorship. In contemporary Malaysia the ethnic cleavages are real, and everyday understanding is a mixture of fantasy and cultural longing. One wants more of what the others have—be it wealth and business talent, or political power and domination. In this context, the hard-working Chinese shopkeeper and his frugal ways become the cornerstone of cultural prejudice and communal self-identity.

In writing the book, I have spent much time with my young sister visiting relatives, trying to get a grip on our parents' inner life. We went about in her car with a driver. The driver freed us from having to find a parking space in the crowded city streets, and dropped us right in front of the shop one of our kin was running. At the shop we talked and I wrote on my notebook. Afterwards I wandered around the shop, and took a chair near the shopfront. The scene I saw was almost a cliché: the shopboys in their sweaty sport shirts, the boss' keen eyes and firm voices, the ceiling fan listlessly turning, the children doing homework on a small table at the corner. It brought up an unbearable sense of nostalgia. It jigged the memory: this was where I came from; this was where it all began. What I am owes a good deal to an Asian shophouse like this one.

I have, unfairly, insisted on the futility of the petite capitalist dream that prevails among the Chinese shophouses. Not every shopkeeper is a Willy Loman figure, fallible and tragic. Like Simmel's idea of money and modern culture, petite capitalism can be double-faced, both constricting and liberating for the individual. Who is to say the petite bourgeoise values would not propel a child towards achievement, towards overcoming his or her legacy of penury. I remember James Scott's slim chapter in *Two Cheers for Anarchism*.[15] 'Two cheers for the petty bourgeoisie' makes an argument that is part economic determinism, part cultural making. The livelihood of petty traders and small land holders make them treasure independence and distrust bureaucracy and big institutions. They live and work 'small', so are the rewards and returns of their labour. However, a certain pride—a certain culture of rebelliousness—gloss what they do and believe in. The pride of work and economic ownership is a classic petite bourgeoise trait. It has given dignity to the army of shopkeepers and traders and back-lane operators. The Pho Restaurant down the road from my Sydney house is run by an ex-major of the South Vietnamese Army, who said to me: When I arrived in Australia after two years in a Malaysian refugee camp, I got a job in garage working for other people. I lasted a month before I resigned. I later set up my own business. He made me think of my father: even with the tedium of day in and day out in the family shop, he was not under anyone's thumb. Dignity is not too grand a term to describe the good sense, the virtue, of the petite capitalist's need to work for oneself.

At the Chopstick Restaurant, I was a long way from home. The family circumstances had radically changed, and I was three years into my Economics degree. Everything made me pause and revaluate what I had gone through, and what lay ahead. Perhaps that's why I was happy at the restaurant, with its boiling wok and the scene of Weegee-like depredation. Looking back, I think now the sense of self-worth and independence I had felt was near enough to be the anarchist's defiance that Scott talks about. If nothing else, it has made me hang on to what I remember of that young man who became his own person in a Chinese takeaway. I am also thinking: Chinese petite capitalism may not be a bad legacy to live up to for anyone.

## Notes

1. Susan Sontag, *Illness as Metaphor*, New York: Farrar and Giroux, 1978, p. 3.
2. Ibid., pp. 3–4.
3. For the cultural principles of Chinese funeral, see: H.G.H. Nelson, 'Ancestral worship and burial practices', in Arthur P. Wolf (ed), *Religion*

*and Ritual in Chinese Society*, Stanford, CA: Stanford University, 1973, pp. 251–278.
4. See: George E. Marcus, *Lives in Trust: The Fortunes of Dynastic Families in Late Twentieth-Century America*. Boulder, CO: Westview, 1992.
5. Victor Zheng, 'Inheritance, Chinese Family Business and Economic Development in Hong Kong'. *Journal of Enterprise Culture* 10 (4), 2002, p. 288.
6. Ibid., pp. 287–312.
7. Ibid., p. 307.
8. George E. Marcus, *Lives in Trust*, p. 108.
9. Ibid.
10. Zheng, 'Inheritance, Chinese Family Business and Economic Development in Hong Kong', pp. 298.
11. Georg Simmel, 'The Adventure', translated by David Kettler, in Kurt H. Wolff (ed) *Georg Simmel 1858–1958*, Columbus, OH: Ohio State University Press, 1958, p. 222.
12. Georg Simmel, *The Philosophy of Money*, David Frisby (ed), London and New York: Routledge, 2005.
13. Ibid., p. 394.
14. Georg Simmel, *Simmel on Culture: Selected Writings*, David Frisby and Mike Featherstone (eds), London: Sage, p. 242.
15. James C. Scott, *Two Cheers for Anarchism*, Princeton, NJ: Princeton University Press, 2012, p. 112.

## Bibliography


Georg Simmel, *Simmel on Culture: Selected Writings*, David Frisby and Mike Featherstone (eds), London: Sage.

Marcus, George E. 1992. *Lives in Trust: The Fortunes of Dynastic Families in Late Twentieth-Century America*. Boulder, CO: Westview Press.

Simmel, Georg. 1958. 'The Adventure', translated by David Kettler, in Kurt H. Wolff (ed) *Georg Simmel 1858–1958*. Columbus, OH: Ohio State University Press, pp. 243–258.

Simmel, Georg. 2005. *The Philosophy of Money*, David Frisby (ed), London and New York: Routledge.

Scott, James C. 2012. *Two Cheers for Anarchism*, Princeton, NJ: Princeton University Press.

Nelson, H.G.H. 1973. 'Ancestral worship and burial practices', in Arthur P. Wolf (ed), *Religion and Ritual in Chinese Society*, Stanford, CA: Stanford University, pp. 251–278.

Sontag, Susan. 1978. *Illness as Metaphor*, New York: Farrar and Giroux.

Zheng, Victor. 2002. 'Inheritance, Chinese Family Business and Economic Development in Hong Kong', *Journal of Enterprise Culture* 10 (4): 287–312.

# Index[1]



[1] Note: Page numbers followed by 'n' refer to notes.




S. Yao, *The Shop on High Street*,
https://doi.org/10.1007/978-981-15-2031-0

The manufacturer's authorised representative in the EU is Springer Nature Customer Service Centre GmbH, Europaplatz 3, 69115 Heidelberg, Germany. If you have any concerns regarding our products, please contact ProductSafety@springernature.com

Printed and bound by CPI Group (UK) Ltd, Croydon, CR0 4YY
25/09/2026
02222902-0017